# THE
# HACKER'S
# HANDBOOK

# THE
# HACKER'S
# HANDBOOK

## HUGO CORNWALL

First published in Great Britain in 1985
by Century Communications Ltd
Portland House, 12-13 Greek Street,
London W1V 5LE

Reprinted 1985 (twice)

ISBN 0 7126 0650 5

Printed and bound in Great Britain
by Billing & Sons Limited, Worcester.

# CONTENTS

# INTRODUCTION

The word 'hacker' is used in two different but associated ways: for some, a hacker is merely a computer enthusiast of any kind, who loves working with the beasties for their own sake, as opposed to operating them in order to enrich a company or research project — or to play games.

This book uses the word in a more restricted sense: hacking is a recreational and educational sport. It consists of attempting to make unauthorised entry into computers and to explore what is there. The sport's aims and purposes have been widely misunderstood; most hackers are *not* interested in perpetrating massive frauds, modifying their personal banking, taxation and employee records, or inducing one world super-power into inadvertantly commencing Armageddon in the mistaken belief that another super-power is about to attack it.    Every hacker I have ever come across has been quite clear about where the fun lies: it is in developing an understanding of a system and finally producing the skills and tools to defeat it. In the vast majority of cases, the process of 'getting in' is much more satisfying than what is discovered in the protected computer files.

In this respect, the hacker is the direct descendant of the phone phreaks of fifteen years ago. Phone phreaking became interesting as intra-nation and international subscriber trunk dialling was introduced, but when the London-based phreak finally chained his way through to Hawaii, he usually had no one there to speak to except the local weather service or American Express office, to confirm that the desired target had indeed been hit. One of the earliest of the present generation of hackers, Susan Headley, only 17 when she began her exploits in California in 1977, chose as her target the local phone company and, with the information extracted from her hacks, ran all over the telephone network. She 'retired' four years later, when friends started developing schemes to shut down part of the phone system.

There is also a strong affinity with program copy-protection crunchers. Most commercial software for micros is sold in a form to prevent obvious casual copying, say by loading a cassette, cartridge or disk into memory and then executing a 'save' on to a blank cassette or disk. Copy-protection devices vary greatly in their methodology and sophistication and there are those who, without any commercial motive, enjoy nothing so much as defeating them. Every computer buff has met at least one cruncher with a vast store of commercial programs, all of which have somehow had the protection removed — and perhaps the main title subtly altered to show the cruncher's technical skills — but which are then never actually *used* at all.

Perhaps I should tell you what you can reasonably expect from this handbook. Hacking is an activity like few others: it is semi-legal, seldom encouraged, and in its full extent so vast that no individual or group, short of an organisation like GCHQ or NSA, could hope to grasp a fraction of the possibilities. So this is not one of those books with titles like *Games Programming with the 6502* where, if the book is any good and if you are any good, you will emerge with some mastery of the subject-matter. The aim of this book is merely to give you some grasp of methodology, help you develop the appropriate attitudes and skills, provide essential background and some referencing material — and point you in the right directions for more knowledge. Up to a point, each chapter may be read by itself; I have compiled extensive appendices, containing material which will be of use long after the main body of the text has been absorbed.

It is one of the characteristics of hacking anecdotes, like those relating to espionage exploits, that almost no one closely involved has much stake in the truth; victims want to describe damage as minimal, and perpetrators like to paint themselves as heroes while carefully disguising sources and methods. In addition, journalists who cover such stories are not always sufficiently competent to write accurately, or even to know when they are being hoodwinked. (A note for journalists: any hacker who offers to break into a system on demand is conning you — the most you can expect is a repeat performance for your benefit of what a hacker has previously succeeded in doing. Getting to the 'front page' of a service or network need not imply that everything within that service can be accessed. Being able to retrieve confidential information, perhaps credit ratings, does not mean that the hacker would also be able to alter that data. Remember the first rule of good reporting: be sceptical.) So far as possible, I have tried to verify each story that appears in these pages, but hackers work in isolated groups and my sources on some of the important hacks of recent years are more remote than I would have liked. In these cases, my accounts are of events and methods which, in all the circumstances, I believe are true. I welcome notes of correction.

Experienced hackers may identify one or two curious gaps in the range of coverage, or less than full explanations; you can chose any combination of the following explanations without causing me any worry: first, I may be ignorant and incompetent; second, much of the fun of hacking is making your own discoveries and I wouldn't want to spoil that; third, maybe there are a few areas which are really best left alone.

Nearly all of the material is applicable to readers in all countries; however, the author is British and so are most of his experiences.

The pleasures of hacking are possible at almost any level of computer competence beyond rank beginner and with quite mininimal equipment. It is quite difficult to describe the joy of using the world's cheapest micro, some clever firmware, a home-brew acoustic coupler and find that, courtesy of a friendly remote PDP11/70, you can be playing with Unix, the fashionable multi-tasking operating system.

The assumptions I have made about you as a reader are that you own a modest personal computer, a modem and some communications software which you know, roughly, how to use. (If you are not confident yet, practise logging on to a few hobbyist bulletin boards.) For more advanced hacking, better equipment helps; but, just as very tasty photographs can be taken with snap-shot cameras, the computer equivalent of a Hasselblad with a trolley-load of accessories is not essential.

Since you may at this point be suspicious that I have vast technical resources at my disposal, let me describe the kit that has been used for most of my network adventures. At the centre is a battered old Apple II+, its lid off most of the time to draw away the heat from the many boards cramming the expansion slots. I use an industry standard dot matrix printer, famous equally for the variety of type founts possible, and for the paper-handling path, which regularly skews off. I have two large boxes crammed full of software, as I collect comms software in particular like a deranged philatelist, but I use one package almost exclusively. As for modems — well, at this point the set-up does become unconventional; by the phone point are jack sockets for BT 95A, BT 96A, BT 600 and a North American modular jack. I have two acoustic couplers, devices for plunging telephone handsets into so that the computer can talk down the line, at operating speeds of 300/300 and 75/1200. I also have three heavy, mushroom coloured 'shoe-boxes', representing modem technology of 4 or 5 years ago and operating at various speeds and combinations of duplex/half-duplex. Whereas the acoustic coupler connects my computer to the line by audio, the modem links up at the electrical level and is more accurate and free from error. I have access to other equipment in my work and through friends, but this is what I use most of the time.

Behind me is my other important bit of kit: a filing cabinet. Hacking is *not* an activity confined to sitting at keyboards and watching screens. All good hackers retain formidable collections of articles, promotional material and documentation; read on, and you will see why.

Finally, to those who would argue that a hacker's handbook must be giving guidance to potential criminals, I have two things to say: First, few people object to the sports of clay-pigeon shooting or archery, although rifles, pistols and crossbows have no 'real' purpose other than to kill things — and hackers have their own code of responsibility, too. Second, real hacking is not as it is shown in the movies and on tv, a situation which the publication of this book may do something to correct.

The sport of hacking itself may involve breach of aspects of the law, notably theft of electricity, theft of computer time and unlicensed usage of copyright material; every hacker must decide individually each instance as it arises.

Various people helped me on various aspects of this book; they must all remain unnamed — they know who they are and that they have my thanks.

**HC**

CHAPTER 1

# First Principles

The first hack I ever did was executed at an exhibition stand run by BT's then rather new Prestel service. Earlier, in an adjacent conference hall, an enthusiastic speaker had demonstrated view-data's potential world-wide spread by logging on to Viditel, the infant Dutch service. He had had, as so often happens in the these circumstances, difficulty in logging on first time. He was using one of those sets that displays auto-dialled telephone numbers; that was how I found the number to call. By the time he had finished his third unsuccessful log-on attempt I (and presumably several others) had all the pass numbers. While the BT staff were busy with other visitors to their stand, I picked out for myself a relatively neglected viewdata set. I knew that it was possible to by-pass the auto-dialler with its pre-programmed phone numbers in this particular model, simply by picking up the the phone adjacent to it, dialling my preferred number, waiting for the whistle, and then hitting the keyboard button labelled 'viewdata'. I dialled Holland, performed my little by-pass trick and watched Viditel write itself on the screen. The pass numbers were accepted first time and, courtesy of...no, I'll spare them embarrassment...I had only lack of fluency in Dutch to restrain my explorations. Fortunately, the first BT executive to spot what I had done was amused as well.

Most hackers seem to have started in a similar way. Essentially you rely on the foolishness and inadequate sense of security of computer salesmen, operators, programmers and designers.

In the introduction to this book I described hacking as a sport; and like most sports, it is both relatively pointless and filled with rules, written or otherwise, which have to be obeyed if there is to be any meaningfulness to it. Just as rugby football is not only about forcing a ball down one end of a field, so hacking is not just about using any means to secure access to a computer.

On this basis, opening private correspondence to secure a password on a public access service like Prestel and then running around the system building up someone's bill, is not what hackers call hacking. The critical element must be the use of skill in some shape or form.

1

Hacking is not a new pursuit. It started in the early 1960s when the first "serious" time-share computers began to appear at university sites. Very early on, 'unofficial' areas of the memory started to appear, first as mere noticeboards and scratchpads for private programming experiments, then, as locations for games. (Where, and how do you think the early Space Invaders, Lunar Landers and Adventure Games were created?) Perhaps tech-hacking — the mischievous manipulation of technology — goes back even further. One of the old favourites of US campus life was to rewire the control panels of elevators (lifts) in high-rise buildings, so that a request for the third floor resulted in the occupants being whizzed to the twenty-third.

Towards the end of the 60s, when the first experimental networks arrived on the scene (particularly when the legendary ARPAnet — Advanced Research Projects Agency network — opened up), the computer hackers skipped out of their own local computers, along the packet-switched high grade communications lines, and into the other machines on the net. But all these hackers were privileged individuals. They were at a university or research resource, and they were able to borrow terminals to work with.

What has changed now, of course, is the wide availability of home computers and the modems to go with them, the growth of public-access networking of computers, and the enormous quantity and variety of computers that can be accessed.

Hackers vary considerably in their native computer skills; a basic knowledge of how data is held on computers and can be transferred from one to another is essential. Determination, alertness, opportunism, the ability to analyse and synthesise, the collection of relevant helpful data and luck — the pre-requisites of any intelligence officer — are all equally important. If you can write quick effective programs in either a high level language or machine code, well, it helps. A knowledge of on-line query procedures is helpful, and the ability to work in one or more popular mainframe and mini operating systems could put you in the big league.

The materials and information you need to hack are all around you — only they are seldom marked as such. Remember that a large proportion of what is passed off as 'secret intelligence' is openly available, if only you know where to look and how to appreciate what you find. At one time or another, hacking will test everything you know about computers and communications. You will discover your abilities increase in fits and starts, and you must be prepared for long periods when nothing new appears to happen.

Popular films and tv series have built up a mythology of what hackers can do and with what degree of ease. My personal delight in such Dream Factory output is in compiling a list of all the mistakes in each episode. Anyone who has ever tried to move a graphics game from one micro to an almost-similar competitor will already know that the chances of getting a home micro to display the North Atlantic Strategic Situation as it would be viewed from the President's Command Post would be slim even if appropriate telephone numbers and passwords were available. Less immediately obvious is the fact that most home micros talk to the outside world through limited but convenient asynchronous protocols, effectively denying direct access to the mainframe products of the world's undisputed leading computer manufacturer, which favours synchronous protocols. And home micro displays are memory-mapped, not vector-traced... Nevertheless, it is astonishingly easy to get remarkable results. And thanks to the protocol transformation facilities of PADs in PSS networks (of which much more later), you *can* get into large IBM devices....

The cheapest hacking kit I have ever used consisted of a ZX81, 16K RAMpack, a clever firmware accessory and an acoustic coupler. Total cost, just over £100. The ZX81's touch-membrane keyboard was one liability; another was the uncertainty of the various connectors. Much of the cleverness of the firmware was devoted to overcoming the native drawbacks of the ZX81's inner configuration — the fact that it didn't readily send and receive characters in the industry-standard ASCII code, and that the output port was designed more for instant access to the Z80's main logic rather than to use industry-standard serial port protocols and to rectify the limited screen display.

Yet this kit was capable of adjusting to most bulletin boards; could get into most dial-up 300/300 asynchronous ports, reconfiguring for word-length and parity if needed; could have accessed a PSS PAD and hence got into a huge range of computers not normally availible to micro-owners; and, with another modem, could have got into viewdata services. You could print out pages on the ZX 'tin-foil' printer. The disadvantages of this kit were all in convenience, not in facilities. Chapter 3 describes the sort of kit most hackers use.

It is even possible to hack with no equipment at all. All major banks now have a network of 'hole in the wall' cash machines — ATMs or Automatic Telling Machines, as they are officially

3

known. Major building societies have their own network. These machines have had faults in software design, and the hackers who played around with them used no more equipment than their fingers and brains. More about this later.

Though I have no intention of writing at length about hacking etiquette, it is worth one paragraph: lovers of fresh-air walks obey the Country Code; they close gates behind them, and avoid damage to crops and livestock. Something very similar ought to guide your rambles into other people's computers: don't manipulate files unless you are sure a back-up exists; don't crash operating systems; don't lock legitimate users out from access; watch who you give information to; if you really discover something confidential, keep it to yourself. Hackers should not be interested in fraud. Finally, just as any rambler who ventured past barbed wire and notices warning about the Official Secrets Acts would deserve whatever happened thereafter, there are a few hacking projects which should never be attempted.

On the converse side, I and many hackers I know are convinced of one thing: we receive more than a little help from the system managers of the computers we attack. In the case of computers owned by universities and polys, there is little doubt that a number of them are viewed like academic libraries — strictly speaking they are for the student population, but if an outsider seriously thirsty for knowledge shows up, they aren't turned away. As for other computers, a number of us are almost sure we have been used as a cheap means to test a system's defences...someone releases a phone number and low-level password to hackers (there are plenty of ways) and watches what happens over the next few weeks while the computer files themselves are empty of sensitive data. Then, when the results have been noted, the phone numbers and passwords are changed, the security improved etc etc....much easier on dp budgets than employing programmers at £150/man/day or more. Certainly the Pentagon has been known to form 'Tiger Units' of US Army computer specialists to pin-point weaknesses in systems security.

Two spectacular hacks of recent years have captured the public imagination: the first, the Great Prince Philip Prestel Hack, is described in detail in chapter 8, which deals with viewdata. The second was spectacular because it was carried out on live national television. It occurred on October 2nd 1983 during a follow-up to the BBC's successful Computer Literacy series. It's worth reporting here, because it neatly illustrates the essence of hacking as a sport...skill with systems, careful research, maximum impact with minimum real harm, and humour.

The tv presenter, John Coll, was trying to show off the Telecom Gold electronic mail service. Coll had hitherto never liked long passwords and, in the context of the tight timing and pressures of live tv, a two letter password seemed a good idea at the time. On Telecom Gold, it is only the password that is truly confidential; system and account numbers, as well as phone numbers to log on to the system, are easily obtainable. The BBC's account number, extensively publicised, was OWL001, the owl being the 'logo' for the tv series as well as the BBC computer.

The hacker, who appeared on a subsequent programme as a 'former hacker' and who talked about his activities in general, but did not openly acknowledge his responsibility for the BBC act, managed to seize control of Coll's mailbox and superimpose a message of his own:

Computer Security Error. Illegal access. I hope your television PROGRAMME runs as smoothly as my PROGRAM worked out your passwords! Nothing is secure!

Hackers' Song

"Put another password in,
Bomb it out and try again
Try to get past logging in,
We're hacking, hacking, hacking

Try his first wife's maiden name,
This is more than just a game,
It's real fun, but just the same,
It's hacking, hacking, hacking"

The Nutcracker (Hackers UK)

— — — — — — — — — —

HI THERE, OWLETS, FROM OZ AND YUG
        (OLIVER AND GUY)

After the hack a number of stories about how it had been carried out, and by whom, circulated; it was suggested that the hackers had crashed through to the operating system of the Prime computers upon which the Dialcom electronic mail software

5

resided — it was also suggested that the BBC had arranged the whole thing as a stunt, or alternatively, that some BBC employees had fixed it up without telling their colleagues. Getting to the truth of a legend in such cases is almost always impossible. No one involved has a stake in the truth. British Telecom, with a strong commitment to get Gold accepted in the business community, was anxious to suggest that only the dirtiest of dirty tricks could remove the inherent confidentiality of their electronic mail service. Naturally, the British Broadcasting Corporation rejected any possibility that it would connive in an irresponsible cheap stunt. But the hacker had no great stake in the truth either — he had sources and contacts to protect, and his image in the hacker community to bolster. Never expect *any* hacking anecdote to be completely truthful.

# CHAPTER 2

# Computer-to-Computer Communications

Services intended for access by microcomputers are nowadays usually presented in a very user-friendly fashion: pop in your software disc or firmware, check the connections, dial the telephone number, listen for the tone...and there you are. Hackers, interested in venturing where they are not invited, enjoy no such luxury. They may want to access older services which preceded the modern 'human interface'; they are very likely to travel along paths intended, not for ordinary customers, but for engineers or salesmen; they could be utilising facilities that were part of a computer's commissioning process and have been hardly used since.

So the hacker needs a greater knowledge of datacomms technology than does a more passive computer user, and some feeling for the history of the technology is pretty essential, because of its growth pattern and because of the fact that many interesting installations still use yesterday's solutions.

Getting one computer to talk to another some distance away means accepting a number of limiting factors:

* Although computers can send out several bits of information at once, the ribbon cable necessary to do this is not economical at any great length, particularly if the information is to be sent out over a network — each wire in the ribbon would need switching separately, thus making exchanges prohibitively expensive. So bits must be transmitted one at at time, or serially.

7

- Since you will be using, in the first instance, wires and networks already installed — in the form of the telephone and telex networks — you must accept that the limited bandwidth of these facilities will restrict the rate at which data can be sent. The data will pass through long lengths of wire, frequently being re-amplified, and undergoing degradation as it passes through dirty switches and relays in a multiplicity of exchanges.

- Data must be easily capable of accurate recovery at the far end.

- Sending and receiving computers must be synchronised in their working.

- The mode in which data is transmitted must be one understood by all computers; accepting a standard protocol may mean adopting the speed and efficiency of the slowest.

The present 'universal' standard for data transmission used by microcomputers and many other services uses agreed tones to signify binary 0 and binary 1, the ASCII character set (also known as International Alphabet No 5), and an asynchronous protocol, whereby the transmitting and receiving computers are locked in step every time a character is sent, not just at the beginning of a transmission stream. Like nearly all standards, it is highly arbitrary in its decisions and derives its importance simply from the fact of being generally accepted. Like many standards, too, there are a number of subtle and important variations.

To see how the standard works, how it came about and the reasons for the variations, we need to look back a little into history.

**The Growth of Telegraphy**
The essential techniques of sending data along wires has a history of 150 years, and some of the common terminology of modern data transmission goes right back to the first experiments.

The earliest form of telegraphy, itself the earliest form of electrical message sending, used the remote actuation of electrical relays to leave marks on a strip of paper. The letters of the alphabet were defined by the patterns of 'mark' and 'space'. The terms have come through to the present, to signify binary conditions of '1' and '0' respectively. The first reliable machine for sending letters and figures by this method dates from 1840; the direct successor of that machine, using remarkably unchanged electro-mechanical technology and a 5-bit alphabetic code, is still widely used today, as the telex/teleprinter/teletype. The mark and space have been replaced by holes punched in paper-tape: larger holes for mark, smaller ones for space. Synchronisation between sending and receiving stations is carried out by beginning each letter with a 'start' bit (a space) and concluding it with a 'stop' bit (mark). The 'idle' state of a circuit is thus 'mark'. In effect, therefore, each letter requires the transmission of 7 bits:

. * * . . . * (letter A: . = space; * = mark)

of which the first . is the start bit, the last * is the stop bit and * * . . . is the code for A.

This is the principle means for sending text messages around the world, and the way in which news reports are distributed globally. And, until third-world countries are rich enough to afford more advanced devices, the technology will survive.

### Early computer communications
When, 110 years after the first such machines came on line, the need arose to address computers remotely, telegraphy was the obvious way to do so. No one expected computers in the early 1950s to give instant results; jobs were assembled in batches, often fed in by means of paper-tape (another borrowing from telex, still in use) and then run. The instant calculation and collation of data was then considered quite miraculous. So the first use of data communications was almost exclusively to ensure that the machine was fed with up-to-date information, not for the machine to send the results out to those who might want it; they could wait for the 'print-out' in due course, borne to them with considerable solemnity by the computer experts. Typical communications speeds were 50 or 75 baud. (The baud is the measure of speed of data transmission: specifically, it refers to the number of signal level changes per second and is thus not the same as bits-per-second.)

These early computers were, of course, in today's jargon, single-user/single-task; programs were fed by direct machine coding. Gradually, over the next 15 years, computers spawned multi-user capabilities by means of time-sharing techniques, and their human interface became more 'user-friendly'. With these facilities grew the demand for remote access to computers, and modern data communications began.

Even at the very end of the 1960s when I had my own very first encounter with a computer, the links with telegraphy were still obvious. As a result of happenstance, I was in a Government-run research facility to the south-west of London, and the program I was to use was located on a computer just to the north of Central London; I was sat down in front of a battered teletype — capitals and figures only, and requiring not inconsiderable physical force from my smallish fingers to actuate the keys of my choice. As it was a teletype outputting on to a paper roll, mistakes could not as readily be erased as on a VDU, and since the sole form of error reporting consisted of a solitary ?, the episode was more frustrating than thrilling. VDUs and good keyboards were then far too expensive for 'ordinary' use.

## The telephone network

But by that time all sorts of changes in datacomms were taking place. The telex and telegraphy network, originally so important, had long been overtaken by voice-grade telephone circuits (Bell's invention dates from 1876). For computer communication, mark and space could be indicated by different audio tones, rather than by different voltage conditions. Data traffic on a telex line can operate in only one direction at a time, but, by selecting different pairs of tones, both 'transmitter' and 'receiver' could speak simultaneously — so that in fact, one has to talk about 'originate' and 'answer' instead.

Improved electrical circuit design meant that higher speeds than 50 or 75 baud became possible; there was a move to 110 baud, then 300 and, so far as ordinary telephone circuits are concerned, 1200 baud is now regarded as the top limit.

The 'start' and 'stop' method of synchronising the near and far end of a commmunications circuit at the beginning of each individual letter has been retained, but the common use of the 5-bit Baudot code has been replaced by a 7-bit extended code which allows for many more characters, 128 in fact.

Lastly, to reduce errors in transmission due to noise in the telephone line and circuitry, each letter can be checked by the use of a further bit (the parity bit), which adds up all the bits in the main character and then, depending on whether the result is odd or even, adds a binary 0 or binary 1.

The full modern transmission of a letter in this system, in this case, K, therefore, looks like this:

START-STOP TRANSMISSION OF A DATA CHARACTER

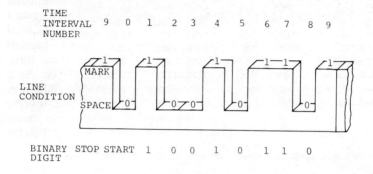

The first 0 is the start bit; then follows 7 bits of the actual letter code (1001011); then the parity bit; then the final 1 is the stop code.

This system, asynchronous start-stop ASCII (the common name for the alphabetic code), is the basis for nearly all micro-based communications. The key variations relate to:

**bit-length**; you can have 7 or 8 databits*

**parity**; (it can be even or odd, or entirely absent),

**tones**. The tones used to signify binary 0 and binary 1, and which computer is in 'originate' and which in 'answer', can vary according to the speed of the transmission and also to whether the service is used in North America or the rest of the world. (Briefly, most of the world uses tones and standards laid down by the Geneva-based organisation, CCITT, a specialised agency of the International Telecommunications Union; whereas in the United States and most parts of Canada, tones determined by the telephone utility, colloquially known as Ma Bell, are adopted.)

The following table gives the standards and tones in common use.

---

*There are no 'obvious explanations' for the variations commonly found: most electronic mail services and viewdata transmit 7 data bits, even parity and 1 stop bit; Telecom Gold and most hobbyist bulletin boards transmit 8 data bits, odd parity and 1 stop bit. Terminal emulator software — see chapter 3 — allows users to adjust for these differing requirements.

| Service Designator | Speed | Duplex | Transmit | | Receive | | Answer |
|---|---|---|---|---|---|---|---|
| | | | 0 | 1 | 0 | 1 | |
| V21 orig | 300* | full | 1180 | 980 | 1850 | 1650 | — |
| V21 ans | 300* | full | 1850 | 1650 | 1180 | 980 | 2100 |
| V23 (1) | 600 | half | 1700 | 1300 | 1700 | 1300 | 2100 |
| V23 (2) | 1200 | f/h† | 2100 | 1300 | 2100 | 1300 | 2100 |
| V23 back | 75 | f/h† | 450 | 390 | 450 | 390 | — |
| Bell 103 orig | 300* | full | 1070 | 1270 | 2025 | 2225 | — |
| Bell 103 ans | 300* | full | 2025 | 2225 | 1070 | 1270 | 2225 |
| Bell 202 | 1200 | half | 2200 | 1200 | 2200 | 1200 | 2025 |

*any speed up to 300 baud, can also include 75 and 110 baud services
†service can either be half-duplex at 1200 baud or asymmetrical full duplex, with 75 baud originate and 1200 baud receive (commonly used as viewdata user) or 1200 transmit and 75 receive (viewdata host)

**Higher Speeds**

1200 baud is usually regarded as the fastest speed possible on an ordinary voice-grade telephone line. Beyond this, noise on the line due to the switching circuits at the various telephone exchanges, poor cabling, etc. make accurate transmission difficult. Indeed, at higher speeds it becomes increasingly important to use transmission protocols that include error correction.

Error correction techniques usually consist of dividing the transmission stream into a series of blocks which can be checked, one at a time, by the receiving computer. The 'parity' system mentioned above is one example, but obviously a crude one. The difficulty is that the more secure an error-correction protocol becomes, the greater becomes the overhead in terms of numbers of bits transmitted to send just one character from one computer to another. Thus, in the typical 300 bit situation, the actual letter is defined by 7 bits, 'start' and 'stop' account for another two, and the check takes a further one — ten in all. After a while, what you gain in the speed with which each actual *bit* is transmitted, you lose, because so many bits have to be sent to ensure that a single *character* is accurately received!

Although some people risk using 2400 baud on ordinary telephone lines — the jargon is the PTSN (Public Telephone Switched Network) — this means using expensive modems. Where higher speeds are essential, leased circuits, not available via dial-up, become essential. The leased circuit is paid for on a fixed charge, not a charge based on time-connected. Such circuits can be 'conditioned', for example by using special amplifiers, to support the higher data rate.

For really high speed transmissions, however, pairs of copper cable are inadequate. Medium speed is obtainable by the use of coaxial cable (a little like that used for tv antenna hook-ups) which have a very broad bandwidth. Imposing several different channels on one cable-length is called multiplexing and, depending on the application, the various channels can either carry several different computer conversations simultaneously or can send several bits of one computer conversation in parallel, just as though there were a ribbon cable between the two participating computers. Either way, what happens is that each binary 0 or binary 1 is given, not an audio tone, but a radio frequency tone.

**Synchronous Protocols**
In the asynchronous protocols so far described, transmitting and receiving computers are kept in step with each other every time a character is sent, via the 'start' and 'stop' bits. In synchronous comms, the locking together is done merely at the start of each block of transmission by the sending of a special code (often SYN). The SYN code starts a clock (a timed train of pulses) in the receiver and it is this that ensures that binary 0s and 1s originating at the transmitter are correctly interpreted by the receiver; clearly, the displacement of even one binary digit can cause havoc.

A variety of synchronous protocols exist, such as the length of block sent each time, the form of checking that takes place, the form of acknowledgement, and so on. A synchronous protocol is not only a function of the modem, which has to have a suitable clock, but also of the software and firmware in the computers. Because asynchronous protocols transmit so many 'extra' bits in order to avoid error, savings in transmission time under synchronous systems often exceed 20–30%. The disadvantage of synchronous protocols lie in increased hardware costs.

One other complication exists: most asynchronous protocols use the ASCII code to define characters. IBM ('Big Blue'), the biggest enthusiast of synchronous comms, has its own binary code to define characters. In Appendix IV, you will find an explanation and a comparison with ASCII.

The hacker, wishing to come to terms with synchronous comms, has two choices: the more expensive is to purchase a protocol convertor board. These are principally available for the IBM PC, which has been increasingly marketed for the 'executive workstation' audience, where the ability to interface to a company's existing (IBM) mainframe is a key feature. The alternative is to see whether the target mainframe has a port on to a packet-switched service; in that event, the hacker can use ordinary asynchronous equipment and protocols — the local PAD (Packet Assembler/Disassembler) will carry out the necessary transformations.

**Networks**
Which brings us neatly to the world of high-speed digital networks using packet-switching. All the computer communications so far described have taken place either on the phone (voice-grade) network or on the telex network.

In Chapter 7 we will look at packet-switching and the opportunities offered by international data networks. We must now specify hackers' equipment in more detail.

# CHAPTER 3

# Hackers' Equipment

You can hack with almost any microcomputer capable of talking to the outside world via a serial port and a modem. In fact, you don't even need a micro; my first hack was with a perfectly ordinary viewdata terminal.

What follows in this chapter, therefore, is a description of the elements of a system I like to think of as optimum for straight-forward asynchronous ASCII and Baudot communications. What is at issue is convenience as much as anything. With kit like this, you will be able to get through most dial-up ports and into packet-switching through a PAD — a packet assembler/disassembler port. (It will not get you into IBM networks, because these use different and incompatible protocols; we will return to the matter of the IBM world in chapter 10.) In other words, given a bit of money, a bit of knowledge, a bit of help from friends and a bit of luck, what is described here is the sort of equipment most hackers have at their command.

You will find few products on the market labelled 'for hackers'; you must select those items that appear to have 'legitimate' but interesting functions and see if they can be bent to the hacker's purposes. The various sections within this chapter highlight the sort of facilities you need; before lashing out on some new software or hardware, try to get hold of as much publicity and documentation material as possible to see how adaptable the products are. In a few cases, it is worth looking at the second-hand market, particularly for modems, cables and test equipment.

Although it is by no means essential, an ability to solder a few connections and scrabble among the circuit diagrams of 'official' products often yield unexpectedly rewarding results.

### The computer

Almost any popular microcomputer will do; hacking does not call upon enormous reserves of computer power. Nearly everything you hack will come to you in alphanumeric form, not graphics. The computer you already have will almost certainly have the essential qualities. However the very cheapest micros, like the ZX81, whilst usable, require much more work on the part of the operator/hacker, and give him far less in the way of instant facilities. (In fact, as the ZX81 doesn't use ASCII internally, but a Sinclair-developed variant; you will need a software or firmware fix for that, before you even think of hooking it up to a modem.)

Most professional data services assume the user is viewing on an 80-column screen; ideally the hacker's computer should be capable of doing that as well, otherwise the display will be full of awkard line breaks. Terminal emulator software (see below) can sometimes provide a 'fix'.

One or two disc drives are pretty helpful, because you will want to be able to save the results of your network adventures as quickly and efficiently as possible. Most terminal emulators use the computer's free memory (i.e. all that is not required to support the operating system and the emulator software itself) as store for the received data, but once the buffer is full, you will begin to lose the earliest items. You can, of course, try to save to cassette, but normally that is a slow and tedious process.

An alternative storage method is to save to a printer, printing the received data stream not only to the computer screen, but also on a dot matrix printer. However, most of the more popular (and cheaper) printers do not work sufficiently fast. You may find you lose characters at the beginning of each line. Moreover, if you print everything in real-time, you'll include all your mistakes, false starts etc., and in the process use masses of paper. So, if you can save to disc regularly, you can review each hack afterwards at your leisure and, using a screen editor or word processor, save or print out only those items of real interest.

### Serial ports
The computer must have a serial port, either called that or marked RS232C (or its slight variant RS423), or V24, which is the official designator of RS232C used outside the USA, though not often seen on micros.

The very cheapest micros, like the ZX81, Spectrum, VIC20, do not have RS232C ports, though add-on boards are available. Some of the older personal computers, like the Apple or the original Pet, were also originally sold without serial ports, though standard boards are available for all of these.

You are probably aware that the RS232C standard has a large number of variants, and that not all computers (or add-on boards) that claim to have a RS232C port can actually talk into a modem.

Historically, RS232C/V24 is supposed to cover all aspects of serial communication, including printers and dumb terminals as well as computers. The RS232C standard specifies electrical and physical requirements. Everything is pumped through a 25-pin D-shaped connector, each pin of which has some function in some implementation. But in most cases, nearly all the pins are not used. In practice, only three connections are essential for computer to modem comunication:

Pin 7    signal ground

Pin 2    characters leaving the computer

Pin 3    characters arriving at the computer

The remaining connections are for such purposes as feeding power to an external device, switching the external advice on or off, exchanging status and timing signals, monitoring the state of the line, and so forth. Some computers and their associated firmware require one or other of these status signals to go 'high' or 'low' in particular circumstances, or the program hangs. Check your documentation if you have trouble.

Some RS232C implementations on microcomputers or add-on boards are there simply to support printers with serial interfaces, but they can often be modified to talk into modems. The critical two lines are those serving Pins 2 and 3.

A computer serving a modem needs a cable in which Pin 2 on the computer is linked to Pin 2 on the modem.

A computer serving a printer, etc, needs a cable in which Pin 3 on the computer is linked to Pin 2 on the printer and Pin 3 on the printer is linked to Pin 2 on the computer.

If two computers are linked together directly, without a modem, then Pin 2 on computer A must be linked to Pin 3 on computer B and Pin 3 on computer B linked to Pin 2 on computer A: this arrangement is sometimes called a 'null modem' or a 'null modem cable'.

There are historic explanations for these arrangements, depending on who you think is sending and who is receiving — forget about them, they are confusing. The above three cases are all you need to know about in practice.

One difficulty that frequently arises with newer or portable computers is that some manufacturers have abandoned the traditional 25-way D-connector, largely on the grounds of bulk, cost and redundancy. Some European computer and peripheral companies favour connectors based on the DIN series (invented in Germany), while others use D-connectors with fewer pin-outs.

*There is no standardization*. Even if you see two physically similar connectors on two devices, regard them with suspicion. In each case, you must determine the equivalents of:

Characters leaving computer (Pin 2)
Characters arriving at computer (Pin 3)
Signal ground (Pin 7)

You can usually set the speed of the port from the computer's operating system and/or from Basic. There is no standard way of doing this; you must check your handbook and manuals. Most RS232C ports can handle the following speeds:

75, 110, 300, 600, 1200, 2400, 4800, 9600

and sometimes 50 and 19200 baud as well. These speeds are selectable in hardware by appropriate wiring of a chip called a baud-rate generator. Many modern computers let you select speed in hardware by means of a DIL switch. The higher speeds are used either for driving printers or for direct computer-to-computer or computer-to-peripheral connections. The normal maximum speed for transmitting along phone lines is 1200 baud.

Depending on how your computer has been set up, you may be able to control the speed from the keyboard — a bit of firmware in the computer will accept micro-instructions to flip transistor switches controlling the wiring of the baud-rate generator. Alternatively, the speeds may be set in pure software, the micro deciding at what speed to feed information into the serial port.

In most popular micro implementations the RS232C cannot support *split-speed* working (different speeds for receive and transmit). If you set the port up for 1200 baud, it has to be 1200 receive and transmit. This is a nuisance in Europe, where 75/1200 is in common use both for viewdata systems and for some on-line services. The usual way round is to have special terminal emulator software, which requires the RS232C hardware to operate at 1200 /1200 and then slows down (usually the micro's transmit path) to 75 baud in software by means of a timing loop. An alternative method relies on a special modem, which accepts data from the computer at 1200/1200 and then performs the slowing-down to 75 baud in its own internal firmware.

**Terminal emulators**
We all need a quest in life. Sometimes I think mine is to search for the perfect software package to make micros talk to the outside

world. As in all such quests, the goal is occasionally approached but never reached, if only because the process of the quest causes one to redefine what one is looking for.

These items of software are sometimes called communications packages, or asynchronous comms packages, and sometimes terminal emulators, on the grounds that the software can make the micro appear to be a variety of different computer terminals. Until recently, most on-line computer services assumed that they were being examined through 'dumb' terminals — simply a keyboard and a screen, with no attendant processing or storage power (except perhaps a printer). With the arrival of PCs all this is slowly changing, so that the remote computer has to do no more than provide relatively raw data and all the formatting and on-screen presentation is done by the user's own computer. Terminal emulator software is a sort of half-way house between 'dumb' terminals and PCs with considerable local processing power.

Given the habit of manufacturers of mainframe and mini-computers to make their products as incompatible with those of their competitors as possible (to maximise their profits), many slight variants on the 'dumb' computer terminal exist — hence the availability of terminal emulators to provide, in one software package, a way of mimicking all the popular types.

Basic software to get a computer to talk through its RS232C port, and to take in data sent to it, is trivial. What the hacker needs is software that will make his computer assume a number of different personalities upon command, store data as it is collected, and print it out.

Two philosophies of presenting such software to the user exist: first, one which gives the naive user a simple menu which says, in effect, 'press a key to connect to database' and then performs everything smoothly, without distracting menus. Such programs need an 'install' procedure, which requires some knowledge, but most 'ordinary' users never see this. Normally, this is a philosophy of software writing I very much admire: however, as a hacker you will want the precise opposite. The second approach to terminal emulator software allows you to reconfigure your computer as you go on — there is plenty of on-screen help in the form of menus allowing you to turn on and off local echo, set parity bits, show non-visible control codes and so on. In a typical hack, you may have only vague information about the target computer, and much of the fun is seeing how quickly you can work out what the remote computer wants to 'see' — and how to make your machine respond.

Given the numbers of popular computers on the market, and

the numbers of terminal emulators for each one, it is difficult to make a series of specific recommendations. What follows therefore, is a list of the sort of facilities you should look for:

*On-line help* You must be able to change the software characteristics while on-line — no separate 'install' routine. You should be able to call up 'help' menus instantly, with simple commands — while holding on to the line.

*Text buffer* The received data should be capable of going into the computer's free memory automatically so that you can view it later off-line. The size of the buffer will depend on the amount of memory left after the computer has used up the space required for its operating system and the terminal software. If the terminal software includes special graphics, as in Apple Visiterm or some of the ROM packs used with the BBC, the buffer space may be relatively small. The software should tell you how much buffer space you have used and how much is left, at any time. A useful adjunct is an auto-save facilitty which, when the buffer becomes full, stops the stream of text from the host computer and automatically saves the buffer text to disc. A number of associated software commands should let you turn on and off the buffer store, clear it or, when off-line, view the buffer. You should also be able to print the buffer to a 'line' printer (dot-matrix or daisy wheel or thermal image). Some terminal emulators even include a simple line editor, so that you can delete or adjust the buffer before printing. (I use a terminal emulator which saves text files in a form which can be accessed by my word-processor and use that before printing out.)

*Half/full Duplex (Echo On/Off)* Most remote services use an echoing protocol: this means that when the user sends a character to the host computer, the host immediately sends back the same character to the user's computer, by way of confirmation. What the user sees on his computer screen, therefore, has been generated, not locally by his direct action on the keyboard, but remotely by the host computer. (One effect of this is that there may sometimes be a perceptible delay between keystroke and display of a letter, particularly if you are using a packet-switched connection — if the telephone line is noisy, the display may appear corrupt). This echoing protocol is known as full duplex, because both the user's computer and the host are in communication simultaneously.

However, use of full duplex/echo is not universal, and all terminal emulators allow you to switch on and off the facility. If, for example, you are talking into a half-duplex system (i.e. no echo), your screen would appear totally blank. In these circumstances, it is best if your software reproduces on the screen your keystrokes. However, if you have your computer set for half-duplex and the host computer is actually operating in full duplex, each letter will appear *twice* — once from the keyboard and once, echoing from the host, ggiivviinngg tthhiiss ssoorrtt ooff eeffffeecctt. Your terminal emulator needs to able to toggle between the two states.

*Data Format/Parity Setting* In a typical asynchronous protocol, each character is surrounded by bits to show when it starts, when it ends, and to signify whether a checksum performed on its binary equivalent comes out even or odd. The character itself is described, typically, in 7 bits and the other bits, start, stop and parity, bringing the number up to 10. (See chapter 2.)

However, this is merely one very common form, and many systems use subtle variants — the ideal terminal emulator software will let you try out these variants *while you are still on line*. Typical variants should include:

| Word length | Parity | No.stop bits |
| --- | --- | --- |
| 7 | even | 2 |
| 7 | odd | 2 |
| 7 | even | 1 |
| 7 | odd | 1 |
| 8 | none | 2 |
| 8 | none | 1 |
| 8 | even | 1 |
| 8 | odd | 1 |

(NB although the ASCII character set is 7 bit, 8 bits are sometimes transmitted with a 'padding' bit; machine code instructions for 8-bit and 16-bit machines obviously need 8-bit transmissions.)

*Show Control Characters* This is a software switch to display characters not normally part of the text that is meant to be read but which nevertheless are sent by the host computer to carry out display functions, operate protocols, etc. With the switch on, you will see line feeds displayed as ↑J, a back-space as ↑H and so on; see Appendix IV for the usual equivalents.

Using this device properly you will be able, if you are unable to get the text stream to display properly on your screen, to work out what exactly is being sent from the host, and modify your local software accordingly. Control-Show is also useful for spotting 'funnies' in passwords and log-on procedures — a common trick is to include ↑ H (backspace) in the middle of a log-on so that part of the full password is overwritten. (For normal reading of text, you have Control-Show switched off, as it makes normal reading difficult.)

*Macros* This is the US term, now rapidly being adopted in the UK, for the preformatting of a log-on procedure, passwords etc. Typical connecting procedures to US services like The Source, CompuServe, Dow Jones etc are relatively complicated, compared with using a local hobbyist bulletin board or calling up Prestel. Typically, the user must first connect to a packet-switched service like Telenet or Tymnet (the US commercial equivalents of BT's PSS), specify an 'address' for the host required (a long string of letters and numbers) and then, when the desired service or 'host' is on line, enter password(s) to be fully admitted. The password itself may be in several parts.

The value of the 'macro' is that you can type all this junk in once and then send off the entire stream any time you wish by means of a simple command. Most terminal emulators that have this feature allow you to preformat several such macros.

From the hacker's point of view, the best type of macro facility is one that can be itself addressed and altered in software: supposing you have only part of a password: write a little routine which successively tries *all* the unknowns; you can then let the computer attempt penetration automatically. (You'll have to read the emulator's manual carefully to see if it has software-addressable macros: the only people who need them are hackers, and, as we have often observed, very few out-and-out hacker products exist!)

*Auto-dial* Some modems contain programmable auto-dialers so that frequently-called services can be dialled from a single keyboard command.

Again the advantage to the hacker is obvious — a partly-known telephone number can be located by writing some simple software routine to test the variables.

However, not all auto-dial facilities are equally useful. Some included in US-originated communications software and terminal emulators are for specific 'smart' modems not available elsewhere — and there is no way of altering the software to work with other equipment. In general, each modem that contains an auto-dialer has its own way of requiring instructions to be sent to it. If an auto-dialing facility is important to you, check that your software is configurable to your choice of auto-dial modem.

Another hazard is that certain auto-dialers only operate on the multi-frequency tones method ('touch-tone') of dialling used in large parts of the United States and only very slowly being introduced in other countries. The system widely used in the UK is called 'pulse' dialling. Touch-tone dialling is much more rapid than pulse dialling, of course.

Finally, on the subject of US-originated software, some packages will only accept phone numbers in the standard North American format of: 3-digit area code, 3-digit local code, 4-digit subscriber code. In the UK and Europe the phone number formats vary quite considerably. Make sure that any auto-dial facility you use actually operates on your phone system.

*Format Screen* Most professional on-line and time-share services assume an 80-column screen. The 'format screen' option in terminal emulators may allow you to change the regular text display on your micro to show 80 characters across by means of a graphics 'fiddle'; alternatively, it may give you a more readable display of the stream from the host by forcing line feeds at convenient intervals, just before the stream reaches the right-hand margin of the micro's 'natural' screen width.

Related to this are settings to handle the presentation of the cursor and to determine cursor movement about the screen — normally you won't need to use these facilities, but they may help you when on-line to some odd-ball, non-standard service. Certain specific 'dumb' terminals like the VT52 (which has become something of a mainframe industry standard) use special sequences to move the cursor about the screen — useful when the operator is filling in standard forms of information.

Other settings within this category may allow you to view characters on your screen which are not part of the normal character set. The early Apples, for example, lacked lower case, presenting everything in capitals (as does the ZX81), so various ingenious 'fixes' were needed to cope. Even quite advanced home computers may lack some of the full ASCII character set, such oddities as the tilde ˜ or backslash \ or curly bracket { } , for example.

*Re-assign keyboard* A related problem is that home micro keyboards may not be able to generate all the required characters the remote service wishes to see. The normal way to generate an ASCII character not available from the keyboard is from Basic, by using a Print CHR$(n) type command. This may not be possible when on-line to a remote computer, where everything is needed in immediate mode. Hence the requirement for a software facility to re-assign any little-used key to send the desired 'missing' feature. Typical requirements are BREAK, ESC, RETURN (when part of a string as opposed to being the end of a command) etc. When re-assigning a series of keys, you must make sure you don't interfere with the essential functioning of the terminal emulator. For example, if you designate the sequence ctrl-S to mean 'send a DC1 character to the host', the chances are you will stop the host from sending anything to you, because ctrl-S is a common command (sometimes called XOF) to call for a pause — incidentally, you can end the pause by hitting ctrl-Q. Appendix IV gives a list of the full ASCII implementation and the usual 'special' codes as they apply to computer-to-computer communications.

*File Protocols* When computers are sending large files to each other, a further layer of protocol, beyond that defining individual letters, is necessary. For example, if your computer is automatically saving to disk at regular intervals as the buffer fills up, it is necessary to be able to tell the host to stop sending for a period, until the save is complete. On older time-share services, where the typical terminal is a teletypewriter, the terminal is in constant danger of being unable mechanically to keep up with the host computer's output. For this reason, many host computers use one of two well-known protocols which require the regular exchange of special control characters for host and user to tell each other all is well. The two protocols are:

*Stop/Start* The receiving computer can at any time send to the host a Stop (ctrl-S) signal, followed by, when it is ready a Start, (ctrl-Q)

*EOB/ACK* The sending computer divides its file into a blocks (of any convenient length); after each block is sent, an EOB (End of Block) character is sent (see ASCII table, Appendix IV). The user's computer must then respond with a ACK (Acknowledge) character.

These protocols can be used individually, together or not at all. You may be able to to use the 'Show Control Codes' option to check whether either of the protocols are in use. Alternatively, if you have hooked on to a service which for no apparent reason, seems to stop in its tracks, you could try ending an ACK or Start (ctrl-F or ctrl-S) and see if you can get things moving.

*File transmission* All terminal emulators assume you will want to send, as well as receive, text files. Thus, in addition to the protocol settings already mentioned, there may be additional ones for that purpose, e.g. the XMODEM protocol very popular on bulletin boards. Hackers, of course, usually don't want to place files *on* remote computers.....

*Specific terminal emulation* Some software has pre-formatted sets of characteristics to mimic popular commercial 'dumb' terminals. For example, with a ROM costing under £60 fitted to a BBC micro, you can obtain almost all of the features of DEC's VT100 terminal, which until recently was regarded as something of an industry-standard and costing just under £1000. Other popular terminals are the VT52 and some Tektronix models, the latter for graphics display. ANSI have produced a 'standard' specification.

*Baudot characters* The Baudot code, or International Telegraphic Code No 2, is the 5-bit code used in telex and telegraphy — and in many wire-based news services. A few terminal emulators include it as an option, and it is useful if you are attempting to hack such services. Most software intended for use on radio link-ups (see Chapter 10) operates primarily in Baudot, with ASCII as an option.

*Viewdata emulation* This gives you the full, or almost full, graphics and text characters of UK-standard viewdata. Viewdata tv sets and adapters use a special character-generator chip and a few, mostly British-manufactured, micros use that chip also — the Acorn Atom was one example. The BBC has a teletext mode which adopts the same display. But for most micros, viewdata emulation is a matter of using high-res graphics to mimic the qualities of the real thing, or to strip out most of the graphics. Viewdata works on a screen 40 characters by 24 rows, and as some popular home micros have 'native' displays smaller than that, some considerable fiddling is necessary to get them to handle viewdata at all.

In some emulators, the option is referred to as Prestel or Micronet — they are all the same thing. Micronet-type software usually has additional facilities for fetching down telesoftware programs (see Chapter 10).

Viewdata emulators must attend not only to the graphics presentation, but also to split-speed operation: the usual speeds are 1200 receive from host, 75 transmit to host. USA users of such services may get them via a packet-switched network, in which case they will receive it either at 1200/1200 full duplex or at 300/300.

Integrated terminal emulators offering both 'ordinary' asynchronous emulation and viewdata emulation are rare: I have to use completely different and non-compatible bits of software on my own home set-up.

## Modems

Every account of what a modem is and does begins with the classic explanation of the derivation of the term: let this be no exception. Modem is a contraction of modulator-demodulator.

A modem taking instructions from a computer (pin 2 on RS232C) converts the binary 0s and 1s into specific single tones, according to which 'standard' is being used. In RS232C/V24, binary 0 (ON) appears as positive volts and binary 1 (OFF) appears as negative volts. The tones are then fed, either acoustically via the telephone mouth-piece into the telephone line, or electrically, by generating the electrical equivalent direct onto the line. This is the modulating process.

In the demodulating stage, the equipment sits on the phone line listening for occurrences of pre-selected tones (again according to whichever 'standard' is in operation) and, when it hears one, delivers a binary 0 or binary 1 in the form of positive or negative voltage pulses into pin 3 of the computer's serial port.

This explanation holds true for modems operating at up to 1200 baud; above this speed, the modem must be able to originate tones, and detect them according to *phase* as well, but since higher-speed working is unusual in dial-up ports — the hacker's special interest, we can leave this matter to one side.

The modem is a relatively simple bit of kit: on the transmit side it consists of a series of oscillators acting as tone generators, and on receive has a series of narrow band-pass filters. Designers of modems must ensure that unwanted tones do not leak into the telephone line (exchanges and amplifiers used by telephone companies are sometimes remotely controlled by the injection of specific tones) and also that, on the receive side, only the distinct tones used for communications are 'interpreted' into binary 0s or 1s. The other engineering requirements are that unwanted electrical currents do not wander down the telephone cable (to the possible risk of phone company employees) or back into the user's computer.

Until relatively recently, the only UK source of low-speed modems was British Telecom. The situation is much easier now, but de-regulation of 'telephone line attachments', which include modems, is still so recent that the ordinary customer can easily become confused. Moreover, modems offering exactly the same service can vary in price by over 300%. Strictly speaking, all modems connected to the phone line should be officially approved by BT or other appropriate regulatory authority.

At 300 baud, you have the option of using direct-connect modems which are hard-wired into the telephone line, an easy enough exercise, or using an acoustic coupler in which you place the telephone hand-set. Acoustic couplers are inherently prone to interference from room-noise, but are useful for quick lash-ups and portable operation. Many acoustic couplers operate only in 'originate' mode, not in' answer'. Newer commercial direct-connect modems are cheaper than acoustic couplers.

At higher speeds acoustic coupling is not recommended, though a 75/1200 acoustic coupler produced in association with the Prestel Micronet service is not too bad, and is now exchanged on the second-hand market very cheaply indeed.

I prefer modems that have proper status lights — power on, line seized, transmit and receive indicators. Hackers need to know what is going on more than most users.

The table below shows all but two of the types of service you are likely to come across; V-designators are the world-wide 'official' names given by the CCITT; Bell-designators are the US names:

| Service Designator | Speed | Duplex | Transmit 0 | Transmit 1 | Receive 0 | Receive 1 | Answer |
|---|---|---|---|---|---|---|---|
| V21 orig | 300* | full | 1180 | 980 | 1850 | 1650 | — |
| V21 ans | 300* | full | 1850 | 1650 | 1180 | 980 | 2100 |
| V23 (1) | 600 | half | 1700 | 1300 | 1700 | 1300 | 2100 |
| V23 (2) | 1200 | f/h† | 2100 | 1300 | 2100 | 1300 | 2100 |
| V23 back | 75 | f/h† | 450 | 390 | 450 | 390 | — |
| Bell 103 orig | 300* | full | 1070 | 1270 | 2025 | 2225 | — |
| Bell 103 ans | 300* | full | 2025 | 2225 | 1070 | 1270 | 2225 |
| Bell 202 | 1200 | half | 2200 | 1200 | 2200 | 1200 | 2025 |

*any speed up to 300 baud can also include 75 and 110 baud services
†service can either be half-duplex at 1200 baud or asymmetrical full duplex, with 75 baud originate and 1200 baud receive (commonly used as viewdata user) or 1200 transmit and 75 receive (viewdata host)

The two exceptions are:
V22          1200 baud full duplex, two wire
Bell 212A  The US equivalent
These services use phase modulation as well as tone.

British Telecom markets the UK services under the name of Datel — details are given in Appendix V.

BT's methods of connecting modems to the line are either to hard-wire the junction box (the two outer-wires are the ones you usually need) — a 4-ring plug and associated socket (type 95A) for most modems, a 5-ring plug and associated socket (type 96A) for

Prestel applications (note that the fifth ring isn't used) — and, for all new equipment, a modular jack called type 600. The US also has a modular jack, but of course it is not compatible.

Modern modem design is greatly aided by a wonder chip called the AMD 7910. This contains nearly all the facilities to modulate and demodulate the tones associated with the popular speed services, both in the CCITT and Bell standards. The only omission — not always made clear in the advertisements — are services using 1200/1200 full-duplex, ie V22 and Bell 212A.

Building a modem is now largely a question of adding a few peripheral components, some switches and indicator lights, and a box. In deciding which 'world standard' modem to purchase, hackers should consider the following features:

*Status lights* you need to be able to see what is happening on the line

*Hardware/software switching* cheaper versions merely give you a switch on the front enabling you to change speeds, originate or answer mode and CCITT or Bell tones. More expensive ones feature firmware which allows your computer to send specially formatted instructions to change speed under program control. However, to make full use of this facility, you may need to write (or modify) your terminal emulator.

*Auto-dial* a pulse dialler and associated firmware are included in some more expensive models. You should ascertain whether the auto-dialer operates on the telephone system you intend to hook the modem up to — some of the US 'smart' modems present difficulties outside the States. You will of course need software in your micro to address the firmware in the modem — and the software has to be part of your terminal emulator, otherwise you gain nothing in convenience. However, with appropriate software, you can get your computer to try a whole bank of numbers one after the other.

*D25 connector* this is the official 'approved' RS232C/V24 physical connection — useful from the point-of-view of easy hook-up. A number of lower-cost models substitute alternative DIN connectors. You must be prepared to solder up your own cables to be sure of connecting up properly.

*Documentation* I always prefer items to be accompanied by proper instructions. Since hackers tend to want to use equipment in unorthodox ways, they should look for good documentation too.

Finally, a word on build-your-own modems. A number of popular electronics magazines and mail-order houses have offered modem designs. Such modems are not likely to be approved for direct connection to the public telephone network. However, most of them work. If you are uncertain of your kit-constructing skills, though, remember badly-built modems can be dangerous both to your computer and to the telephone network.

## Test Equipment

Various items of useful test equipment occasionally appear on the second-hand market — via mail-order, in computer junk shops, in the flea-market section of exhibitions and via computer clubs.

It's worth searching out a cable 'break-out' box. This lets you restrap a RS232C cable without using a soldering iron — the various lines are brought out on to an accessible matrix and you use small connectors to make (or break) the links you require. It's useful if you have an 'unknown' modem, or an unusually configured computer.

Related, but much more expensive, is a RS232C/V24 analyser — this gives LED status lights for each of the important lines, so you can see what is happening.

Lastly, if you are a very rich and enthusiastic hacker, you can buy a protocol analyser. This is usually a portable device with a VDU, full keyboard, and some very clever firmware which examines the telephone line or RS232C port and carries out tests to see which of several popular datacomms protocols is in use. Hewlett Packard do a nice range. Protocol analysers will handle synchronous transmissions as well as synchronous. Cost: £1500 and up...and up.

CHAPTER 4

# Targets

Wherever hackers gather, talk soon moves from past achieve-
ments and adventures to speculation about what new territory
might be explored. It says much about the compartmentalisation
of computer specialities in general and the isolation of micro-
owners from mainstream activities in particular that a great deal of
this discussion is like that of navigators in the days before
Columbus: the charts are unreliable, full of blank spaces and
confounded with myth.

In this chapter I am attempting to provide a series of notes on
the main types of services potentially available on dial-up, and to
give some idea of the sorts of protocols and conventions
employed. The idea is to give voyagers an outline atlas of what is
interesting and possible, and what is not.

### On-line hosts

On-line services were the first form of electronic publishing: a
series of big storage computers — and on occasion, associated
dedicated networks — act as hosts to a group of individual
databases by providing not only mass data storage and the
appropriate 'search language' to access it, but also the means for
registering, logging and billing users. Typically, users access the
on-line hosts via a phone number which links into a a public data
network using packet switching (there's more on these networks in
chapter 7).

The on-line business began almost by accident; large corporations and institutions involved in complicated technological
developments found that their libraries simply couldn't keep track
of the publication of relevant new scientific papers, and decided to
maintain indices of the papers by name, author, subject-matter,
and so on, on computer. One of the first of these was the
armaments and aircraft company, Lockheed Corporation.

In time the scope of these indices expanded and developed and
outsiders — sub-contractors, research agencies, universities,
government employees, etc were granted access. Other organisations with similar information-handling requirements asked if
space could be found on the computer for their needs. Eventually

Lockheed and others recognised the beginnings of a quite separate business; in Lockheed's case it lead to the foundation of Dialog, which today acts as host and marketing agent for almost 300 separate databases. Other on-line hosts include BRS (Bibliographic Retrieval Services), Comshare (used for sophisticated financial modelling), DataStar, Blaise (British Library), I P Sharp, and Euronet-Diane.

On-line services, particularly the older ones, are not especially user-friendly by modern standards. They were set up at a time when both core and storage memory was expensive, and the search languages tend to be abbreviated and formal. Typically they are used, not by the eventual customer for the information, but by professional intermediaries — librarians and the like — who have undertaken special courses. Originally on-line hosts were accessed by dumb terminals, usually teletypewriters like the Texas Whisperwriter portable with built-in acoustic modem, rather than by VDUs. Today the trend is to use 'front-end' intelligent software on an IBM PC which allows the naive user to pose his/her questions informally while offline; the software then redefines the information request into the formal language of the on-line host (the user does not witness this process) and then goes on-line via an auto-dial modem to extract the information as swiftly and efficiently as possible.

On-line services require the use of a whole series of passwords: the usual NUI and NUA for PSS (see chapter 7), another to reach the host, yet another for the specific information service required. Charges are either for connect-time or per record retrieved, or sometimes a combination.

The categories of on-line service include *bibliographic*, which merely indexes the existence of an article or book — you must then find a physical copy to read; and *source*, which contains the article or extract thereof. *Full-text* services not only contain the complete article or book but will, if required, search the entire text (as opposed to mere keywords) to locate the desired information. An example of this is LEXIS, a vast legal database which contains nearly all important US and English law judgments, as well as statutes.

**News Services**
The vast majority of news services, even today, are not, in the strictest sense, computer-based, although computers play an important role in assembling the information and, depending on the nature of the newspaper or radio or tv station receiving it, its subsequent handling.

The world's big press agencies — United Press, Associated Press, Reuters, Agence France Presse, TASS, Xinhua, PAP, VoA — use telex techniques to broadcast their stories. Permanent leased telegraphy lines exist between agencies and customers, and the technology is pure telex: the 5-bit Baudot code (rather than ASCII) is adopted, giving capital letters only, and 'mark' and 'space' are sent by changing voltage conditions on the line rather than audio tones. Speeds are 50 or 75 baud.

The user cannot interrogate the agency in any way. The stories come in a single stream which is collected on rolls of paper and then used as per the contract between agency and subscriber.

To hack a news agency line you will need to get physically near the appropriate leased line, tap in by means of an inductive loop, and convert the changing voltage levels ($\pm 80$ volts on the line) into something your RS232C port can handle. You will then need software to translate the Baudot code into the ASCII which your computer can handle internally, and display on screen or print to a file. The Baudot code is given in Appendix IV.

None of this is easy and will probably involve breaches of several laws, including theft of copyright material! However a number of news agencies also transmit services by radio, in which case the signals can be hijacked with a short-wave receiver. Chapter 9 explains.

Historic news, as opposed to the current stuff from agencies, is now becoming available on-line. *The New York Times*, for example, has long held its stories in an electronic 'morgue' or clippings library. Initially this was for internal use, but for the last several years it has been sold to outsiders, chiefly broadcasting stations and large corporations. You can search for information by a combination of keyword and date-range. *The New York Times* Information Bank is available through several on-line hosts.

As the world's great newspapers increasingly move to electronic means of production — journalists working at VDUs, sub-editors assembling pages and direct-input into photo-typesetters — the additional cost to each newspaper of creating its own morgue is relatively slight and we can expect to see many more commercial services.

In the meantime, other publishing organisations have sought to make available articles, extract or complete, from leading magazines also. Two UK examples are Finsbury Data Services' Textline and Datasolve's World Reporter, the latter including material from the BBC's monitoring service, Associated Press, the *Economist* and the *Guardian*. Textline is an abstract service, but World Reporter gives the full text. In October 1984 it already held

500 million English words. In the US there is NEXIS, which shares resources with LEXIS; NEXIS held 16 million full text articles at that same date. All these services are expensive for casual use and are accessed by dial-up using ordinary asynchronous protocols.

Many electronic newsrooms also have dial-in ports for reporters out on the job; depending on the system these ports not only allow the reporter to transmit his or her story from a portable computer, but may also (like Basys Newsfury used by Channel Four News) let them see news agency tapes, read headlines and send electronic mail. Such systems have been the subject of considerable hacker speculation.

### Financial Services

The financial world can afford more computer aids than any other non-governmental sector. The vast potential profits that can be made by trading huge blocks of currency, securities or commod-ities — and the extraordinary advantages that a slight 'edge' in information can bring — have meant that the City, Wall Street and the equivalents in Hong Kong, Japan and major European capitals have been in the forefront of getting the most from high-speed comms.

Ten years ago the sole form of instant financial information was the ticker tape — telegraphy technology delivering the latest share price movements in a highly abbreviated form. As with its news equivalents, these were broadcast services (and still are, for the services still exist) sent along leased telegraph lines. The user could only watch, and 'interrogation' consisted of back-tracking along a tape of paper. Extel (Exchange Telegraph) continues to use this technique, though it is gradually upgrading by using viewdata and intelligent terminals.

However, just over ten years ago Reuters put together the first packages which gave some intelligence and 'questioning power' to the end user. Each Reuters' Monitor is intelligent, containing (usually) a DEC PDP-8 series mini and some firmware which accepts and selects the stream of data from the host at the far end of the leased line, marshalls interrogation requests and takes care of the local display. Information is formatted in 'pages' rather like viewdata frames, but without the colour. There is little point in eavesdropping into a Reuters line unless you know what the terminal firmware does. Reuters now face an aggressive rival in Telerate, and the fight is on to deliver not only fast comprehensive prices services but international screen-based dealing as well. The growth of Reuters and its rivals is an illustration of technology creating markets — especially in international currency — where none existed before.

The first sophisticated Stock Exchange prices 'screens' used modified closed circuit television technology. London had a system called Market Price Display Service — MPDS — which consisted of a number of tv displays of current prices services on different 'channels' which could be selected by the user. But London now uses TOPIC, a leased line variant on viewdata technology, though with its magazine-like arrangement and auto-screen refresh, it has as much in common with teletext as Prestel. TOPIC carries about 2,500 of the total 7,500 shares traded in London, plus selected analytical material from brokers. Datastream represents a much higher level of sophistication: using its £40,000 plus pa terminals you can compare historic data — price movements, movements against sector indices etc — and chart the results.

The hacker's reward for getting into such systems is that you can see share and other prices on the move. None of these prices is confidential; all could be obtained by ringing a stockbroker. However, this situation is likely to change; as the City makes the change from the traditional broker/jobber method of dealing towards specialist market making, there will then be electronic prices services giving privileged information to specialist share dealers.

All these services are only available via leased lines; City professionals would not tolerate the delays and uncertainties of dial-up facilities. However dial-up ports exist for demonstrations, exhibitions, engineering and as back-up — and a lot of hacking effort has gone into tracking them down.

In the United States, in addition to Reuters, Telerate and local equivalents of official streams of stock exchange and over-the-counter data, there is Dow Jones, best known internationally for its market indices similar to those produced by the Financial Times in London. Dow Jones is in fact the owner of the Wall Street Journal and some influential business magazines. Its Dow Jones News/Retrieval Service is aimed at businesses and private investors. It features current share prices, deliberately delayed by 15 minutes, historic price data, which can be charted by the user's own computer (typically an Apple or IBM PC) and historic 'morgue' type company news and analysis. Extensions of the service enable customers to examine accounts of companies in which they are interested. The bulk of the information is US-based, but can be obtained world-wide via packet-switching networks. All you need are the passwords and special software.

**Business Information**

Business information is usually about the credit-worthiness of companies, company annual reports, trading opportunities and market research. The biggest electronic credit data resource is owned by the international company Dun & Bradstreet: during 1985-86 it is due to spend £25m on making its data available all over Europe, including the UK. The service, which covers more than 250,000 UK businesses, is called DunsPrint and access is both on-line and via a viewdata front-end processor. Another credit agency, CNN Services, extensively used already by the big clearing banks, and with 3000 customers accessing information via viewdata sets, has recently also announced an extended electronic retrieval service for its own called Guardian Business Information. A third UK credit service available electronically is called InfoLink.

In addition, all UK companies quoted on the London Stock Exchange and many others of any size who are not, have a report and analysis available from ICC (InterCompany Comparisons) who can be accessed via on−line dial−up, through a viewdata interface and also by Datastream customers. Dun & Bradstreet also have an on−line service called KBE covering 20,000 key British enterprises.

Prodigious quantities of credit and background data on US companies can be found on several of the major on−line hosts. A valid phone number, passwords and extracts from the operations manual of one of the largest US services, TRW — it has credit histories on 90 million people — sat on some hackers' bulletin boards (of which much more later) for over twelve months during 1983 and 1984 before the company found out. No one knows how many times hackers accessed the service. According to the *Washington Post*, the password and manual had been obtained from a Sears Roebuck national chain store in Sacramento; some hackers claimed they were able to alter credit records, but TRW maintain that telephone access to their systems is designed for read-only operations alone, updating of files taking place solely on magnetic tape.

US market research and risk analysis comes from Frost & Sullivan. Risk analysis tells international businessmen which countries are politically or economically unstable, or likely to become so, and so unsafe to do business with. I once found myself accessing a viewdata-based international assessment service run by a company called Control Risks, which reputedly has strong links to the Special Air Service. As so often happens when hackers think they are about to uncover secret knowledge, the actual data files seemed relatively trivial, the sort of judgments that could be made by a bright sixth former who read posh newspapers and thoughtful weekly magazines.

## University facilities

In complete contrast to computers that are used to store and present data are those where the value is to deliver processing power to the outside world. Paramount among these are those installed in universities and research institutes.

Although hackers frequently acquire phone numbers to enter such machines, what you can do once you are there varies enormously. There are usually tiers and banks of passwords, each allowing only limited access to the range of services. It takes considerable knowledge of the machine's operating system to break through from one to another and indeed, in some cases, the operating system is so thoroughly embedded in the mainframe's hardware architecture that the substantial modifications necessary to permit a hacker to roam free can only be done from a few designated terminals, or by having physical access to the machine. However, the hobbyist bulletin board system quite often provides passwords giving access to games and the ability to write and run programs in exotic languages — my own first hands–on experience of Unix came in exactly this way. There are bulletin boards on mainframes and even, in some cases, boards for hackers!

Given the nature of hacking, it is not surprising that some of the earliest japes occurred on computers owned by universities. Way back in the 1970s, MIT was the location of the famous 'Cookie Monster', inspired by a character in the then-popular *Rowan & Martin Laugh-In* television show. As someone worked away at their terminal, the word 'cookie' would appear across their screen, at first slowly wiping out the user's work. Unless the user moved quickly, things started to speed up and the machine would flash urgently: "Cookie, cookie, give me a cookie". The whole screen would pulse with this message until, after a while, the hacking program relented and the 'Monster' would clear the screen, leaving the message: "I didn't want a cookie anyway." It would then disappear into the computer until it snared another unsuspecting user. You could save yourself from the Monster by typing the word "Cookie", to which it replied "Thank you" and then vanished.

In another US case, this time in 1980, two kids in Chicago, calling themselves System Cruncher and Vladimir, entered the computer at DePaul University and caused a system crash which cost $22,000 to fix. They were prosecuted, given probation and were then made a movie offer.

In the UK, many important university and research institution computers have been linked together on a special data network called SERCNET. SERC is the Science and Engineering Research Council. Although most of the computers are individually accessible via PSS, SERCNET makes it possible to enter one computer and pass through to others. During early 1984, SERCNET was the target of much hacker attention; a fuller account appears in chapter 7, but to anticipate a little, a local entry node was discovered via one of the London University college computers with a demonstration facility which, if asked nicely, disgorged an operating manual and list of 'addresses'. One of the minor joys of this list was an entry labelled "Gateway to the Universe", pure Hitch-hiker material, concealing an extensive long-term multi-function communications project. Eventually some hackers based at a home counties university managed to discover ways of roaming free around the network....

## Banking

Prominent among public fantasies about hackers is the one where banks are entered electronically, accounts examined and some money moved from one to another. The fantasies, bolstered by under-researched low-budget movies and tv features, arise from confusing the details of several actual happenings.

Most 'remote stealing' from banks or illicit obtaining of account details touch computers only incidentally and involve straight-forward fraud, conning or bribery of bank employees. In fact, when you think about the effort involved, human methods would be much more cost-effective for the criminal. For hackers, however, the very considerable effort that has been made to provide security makes the systems a great challenge in themselves.

In the United Kingdom, the banking scene is dominated by a handful of large companies with many branches. Cheque clearing and account maintenance are conducted under conditions of high security with considerable isolation of key elements; inter-bank transactions in the UK go through a scheme called CHAPS, Clearing House Automatic Payments System, which uses the X.25 packet switching protocols (see chapter 7). The network is based on Tandem machines; half of each machine is common to the network and half unique to the bank. The encryption standard used is the US Data Encryption Standard. Certain parts of the network, relating to the en- and de-cryption of messages, apparently auto-destruct if tampered with. The service started early in 1984. The international equivalent is SWIFT (Society for Worldwide Interbank Financial Transactions); this is also X.25-based and it handles about half-a-million messages a day. If you want to learn someone's balance, the easiest and most reliable way to obtain it is with a plausible call to the local branch. If you want some easy money, steal a cheque book and cheque card and practise signature imitation. Or, on a grander scale, follow the example of the £780,000 kruggerand fraud in the City. Thieves intercepted a telephone call from a solicitor or bank manager to 'authenticate' forged drafts; the gold coins were then delivered to a bogus company.

In the United States, where federal law limits the size of an individual bank's operations and in international banking, direct attacks on banks has been much easier because the technology adopted is much cruder and more use is made of public phone and telex lines. One of the favourite techniques has been to send fake authorisations for money transfers. This was the approach used against the Security National Pacific Bank by Stanley Rifkin and a Russian diamond dealer in Geneva. $10.2m moved from bank to bank across the United States and beyond. Rifkin obtained code numbers used in the bilateral Test Keys. The trick is to spot weaknesses in the cryptographic systems used in such authorisations. The specifications for the systems themselves are openly published; one computer security expert, Leslie Goldberg, was recently able to take apart one scheme — proposed but not actually implemented — and show that much of the 'key' that was supposed to give high level cryptographic security was technically redundant, and could be virtually ignored. A surprisingly full account of his 'perfect' fraud appears in a 1980 issue of the journal *Computer Fraud and Security Bulletin*.

There are, however, a few areas where banking is becoming vulnerable to the less mathematically literate hacker. A number of international banks are offering their big corporation customers special facilities so that their Treasury Departments (which ensure, among other things, that any spare million dollars are not left doing nothing over night but are earning short-term interest) can have direct access to their account details via a PC on dial-up. Again, telebanking is now available via Prestel and some of its overseas imitators. Although such services use several layers of passwords to validate transactions, if those passwords are mis-acquired, since no signatures are involved, the bank account becomes vulnerable.

Finally, the network of ATMs (hole-in-the-wall cash machines) is expanding greatly. As mentioned early in this book, hackers have identified a number of bugs in the machines. None of them, incidentally, lead directly to fraud. These machines allow card-holders to extract cash up to a finite limit each week (usually £100). The magnetic stripe contains the account number, valida-tion details of the owner's PIN (Personal Identity Number), usually 4 digits, and a record of how much cash has been drawn that week. The ATM is usually off-line to the bank's main computer and only goes on-line in two circumstances — first, during business hours, to respond to a customer's 'balance request'; and second, outside regular hours, to take into local memory lists of invalid cards which should not be returned to the customer, and to dump out cheque book and printed statement requests.

Hackers have found ways of getting more than their cash limit each week. The ATMs belonging to one clearing bank could be 'cheated' in this way: you asked for your maximum amount and then, when the transaction was almost completed, the ATM asked you 'Do you want another transaction, Yes/No?' If you responded 'yes' you could then ask for — and get — your credit limit again, and again, and again. The weakness in the system was that the magnetic stripe was not overwritten to show you had had a transaction till it was physically ejected from the machine. This bug has now been fixed.

A related but more bizarre bug resided for a while on the ATMs used by that first bank's most obvious High Street rivals. In that case, you had to first exhaust your week's limit. You then asked for a further sum, say £75. The machine refused but asked if you wanted a further transaction. Then, you slowly decremented the amounts you were asking for by £5...70, 65, 60...and so on, down to £10. You then told the ATM to cancel the last £5 trans-action...and the machine gave you the full £75. Some hackers firmly believe the bug was placed there by the original software writer. This bug too has now been fixed.

Neither of these quirks resulted in hackers 'winning' money from the banks involved; the accounts were in every case, properly debited. The only victory was to beat the system. For the future, I note that the cost of magnetic stripe reader/writers which interface to PCs is dropping to very low levels. I await the first inevitable news reports.

**Electronic Mail**
Electronic mail services work by storing messages created by some users until they are retrieved by their intended recipients. The

ingredients of a typical system are: registration/logging on facilities, storage, search and retrieval, networking, timing and billing. Electronic mail is an easy add-on to most mainframe installations, but in recent years various organisations have sought to market services to individuals, companies and industries where electronic mail was the main purpose of the system, not an add-on.

The system software in widest use is that of ITT-Dialcom; it's the one that runs Telecom Gold. Another successful package is that used in the UK and USA by Easylink, which is supported by Cable & Wireless and Western Union.

In the Dialcom/Telecom Gold service, the assumption is made that most users will want to concentrate on a relatively narrow range of correspondents. Accordingly, the way it is sold is as a series of systems, each run by a 'manager': someone within a company. The 'manager' is the only person who has direct contact with the electronic mail owner and he in turn is responsible for bringing individual users on to his 'system' — he can issue 'mailboxes' direct, determine tariff levels, put up general messages.

In most other services, every user has a direct relationship with the electronic mail company.

The services vary according to their tariff structures and levels; and also in the additional facilities: some offer bi-directional interfaces to telex; and some contain electronic magazines, a little like videotex.

The basic systems tend to be quite robust and hacking is mainly concentrated on second-guessing users IDs. Many of the systems have now sought to increase security by insisting on passwords of a certain length — and by giving users only three or four attempts at logging on before closing down the line. But increasingly their customers are using PCs and special software to automate logging-in. The software packages of course have the IDs nicely pre-stored....

**Government computers**
Among hackers themselves the richest source of fantasising revolves around official computers like those used by the tax and national insurance authorities, the police, armed forces and intelligence agencies.

The Pentagon was hacked in 1983 by a 19-year-old Los Angeles student, Ronald Austin. Because of the techniques he used, a full account is given in the operating systems section of chapter 6. NASA, the Space Agency, has also acknowledged that its e-mail system has been breached and that messages and pictures of Kilroy

40

were left as graffitti. This leaves only one outstanding mega-target, Platform, the global data network of 52 separate systems focussed on the headquarters of the US's electronic spooks, the National Security Agency at Fort Meade, Maryland. The network includes at least one Cray-1, the world's most powerful number-cruncher, and facilities provided by GCHQ at Cheltenham.

Although I know UK phone freaks who claim to have managed to appear on the internal exchanges used by Century House (MI6) and Curzon Street House (MI5) and have wandered along AUTOVON, the US secure military phone network, I am not aware of anyone bold or clever enough to have penetrated the UK's most secure computers.

It must be acknowledged that in general it is far easier to obtain the information held on these machines — and lesser ones like the DVLC (vehicle licensing) and PNC (Police National Computer) — by criminal means than by hacking — bribery, trickery or blackmail, for example. Nevertheless, there is an interesting hacker's exercise in demonstrating how far it is possible to produce details from open sources of these systems, even when the details are supposed to be secret. But this relates to one of the hacker's own secret weapons — thorough research, the subject of the next chapter.

# CHAPTER 5

# Hackers' Intelligence

Of all the features of hacking that mystify outsiders, the first is how the hackers get the phone numbers that give access to the computer systems, and the passwords that open the data. Of all the ways in which hacking is portrayed in films, books and tv, the most misleading is the concentration on the image of the solitary genius bashing away at a keyboard trying to 'break in'.

It is now time to reveal one of the dirty secrets of hacking: there are really two sorts of hacker. For this purpose I will call them the trivial and the dedicated. Anyone can become a trivial hacker: you acquire, from someone else, a phone number and a password to a system; you dial up, wait for the whistle, tap out the password, browse around for a few minutes and log off. You've had some fun, perhaps, but you haven't really done anything except follow a well-marked path. Most unauthorised computer invasions are actually of this sort.

The dedicated hacker, by contrast, makes his or her own discoveries, or builds on those of other pioneers. The motto of dedicated hackers is modified directly from a celebrated split infinitive: to boldly pass where no man has hacked before.

Successful hacking depends on good research. The materials of research are all around: as well as direct hacker-orientated material of the sort found on bulletin board systems and heard in quiet corners during refreshment breaks at computer clubs, huge quantities of useful literature are published daily by the marketing departments of computer companies and given away to all comers: sheaves of stationery and lorry loads of internal documentation containing important clues are left around to be picked up. It is up to the hacker to recognise this treasure for what it is, and to assemble it in a form in which it can be used.

Anyone who has ever done any intelligence work, not necessarily for a government, but for a company, or who has worked as an investigative journalist, will tell you that easily 90% of the information you want is freely available and that the difficult part is recognising and analysing it. Of the remaining 10%, well over half can usually be inferred from the material you already have, because, given a desired objective, there are usually only a limited number of sensible solutions. You can go further: it is often possible to test your inferences and, having done that, develop further hypotheses. So the dedicated hacker, far from spending all the time staring at a VDU and 'trying things' on the keyboard, is often to be found wandering around exhibitions, attending demonstrations, picking up literature, talking on the phone (voice-mode!) and scavenging in refuse bins.

But for both trivial operator, and the dedicated hacker who wishes to consult with his colleagues, the bulletin board movement has been the single greatest source of intelligence.

## Bulletin Boards

Since 1980, when good software enabling solitary micro-computers to offer a welcome to all callers first became widely available, the bulletin board movement has grown by leaps and bounds. If you haven't logged on to at least one already, now is the time to try. At the very least it will test out your computer, modem and software — and your skills in handling them. Current phone numbers, together with system hours and comms protocol requirements, are regularly published in computer mags; once you have got into one, you will usually find current details of most of the others.

Somewhere on most boards you will find a series of Special Interest Group (SIG) sections and among these, often, will be a Hacker's Club. Entrance to each SIG will be at the discretion of the Sysop, the Bulletin Board owner. Since the BBS software allows the Sysop to conceal from users the list of possible SIGs, it may not be immediately obvious whether a Hacker's section exists on a particular board. Often the Sysop will be anxious to form a view of a new entrant before admitting him or her to a 'sensitive' area. It has even been known for bulletin boards to carry *two* hacker sections: one, admission to which can be fairly easily obtained; and a second, the very existence of which is a tightly-controlled secret, where mutually trusting initiates swap information.

The first timer, reading through a hacker's bulletin board, will find that it seems to consist of a series of discursive conversations between friends. Occasionally, someone may write up a summary for more universal consumption. You will see questions being posed...if you feel you can contribute, do so, because the whole idea is that a BBS is an information exchange. It is considered crass to appear on a board and simply ask 'Got any good numbers?'; if you do, you will not get any answers. Any questions you ask should be highly specific, show that you have already done some ground-work, and make clear that any results derived from the help you receive will be reported back to the board.

Confidential notes to individuals, not for general consumption, can be sent using the E-Mail option on the bulletin board, but remember, *nothing* is hidden from the Sysop.

A flavour of the type of material that can be seen on bulletin boards appears from this slightly doctored excerpt (I have removed some of the menu sequences in which the system asks what you want to do next and have deleted the identities of individuals):

```
Msg#: 3538 *MODEM-SPOT*
01/30/84 12:34:04 (Read 39 Times)
From: xxxxxx xxxxxxxx
To: ALL
Subj: BBC/MAPLIN MODEMS
RE THE CONNECTIONS ON THE BBC/MAPLIN MODEM SETUP, THE CTS PIN IS USEDTO
HANDSHAKE WITH THE RTS PIN E.G. ONE UNIT SENDS RTS (READY TO SEND) AND THE
SECOND UNIT REPLIES CTS (CLEAR TO SEND), USUALLY DONE BY TAKING PIN HIGH. IF
YOU STRAP IT HIGH I WOULD SUGGEST VIA A 4K7 RESISTOR TO THE VCC/+VE RAIL (5V).
IN THE EVENT OF A BUFFER OVERFLOW, THESE RTS/CTS PINS ARE TAKEN LOW AND THIS
STOPS THE DATA TRANSFER. ON A 25WAY D TYPE CONNECTOR TX DATA IS PIN 2
RX DATA IS PIN 3
RTS IS PIN 4
CTS IS PIN 5
GROUND IS PIN 7


ALL THE BEST -- ANY COMMTO xxxxxx xxxxxxxx.
(DATA COMMS ENGINEER)


Msg#: 3570 *MODEM-SPOT*
01/31/84 23:43:08 (Read 31 Times)
From: xxxx xxxxx
To: xxxxxx xxxxxxxx
Subj: REPLY TO MSG# 3538 (BBC/MAPLIN MODEMS)
ON THE BBC COMPUTER IT IS EASIER TO CONNECT THE RTS (READY TO SEND) PIN TO THE
CTS (CLEAR TO SEND) PIN. THIS OVERCOMES THE PROBLEM OF HAND SHAKING.
SINCE THE MAPLIN MODEM DOES NOT HAVE HAND SHAKING.I HAVE PUT MY RTS CTS JUMPER
INSIDE THE MODEM.MY CABLES ARE THEN STANDARD AND CAN BE USED WITH HANDSHAKERS.
REGARDS

Msg#: 3662 *HACKER'S CLUB*
02/04/84 23:37:11 (Read 41 Times)
From: xxx xxxxxxx
To: ALL
Subj: PUBLIC DATA NET
Does anyone gnow what the Public Data Net is? I appear to have access to it,&
I daren't ask what it is!
Also, can anyone tell me more about the Primenet systems... Again, I seem to
have the means,but no info. F'rinstance, I have a relative who logs on to
another Prime Both of our systems are on Primenet, is there any way we can
communicate?
More info to those who want it...

<N>ext msg, <R>eply, or <S>top?
Msg has replies, read now(Y/N)? y

Reply has been deleted

<N>ext msg, <R>eply, or <S>top?

Msg#: 3739 *HACKER'S CLUB*
02/06/84 22:39:06 (Read 15 Times)
From: xxx xxxxxxx
To: xxx xxxx
Subj: REPLY TO MSG# 3716 (PRIMENET COMMS)
Ahh, but what is the significance of the Address-does it mean a PSS number, or
some thing like that? Meanwhile,I'll get on-line (via voice-link on the phone!)
to my cousin, and see what he has on it....
```

Msg#: 3766 *HACKER'S CLUB*
02/07/84 13:37:04 (Read 13 Times)
From: xxxxxx xxx
To: xxxxx xxxxxxxxx
Subj: REPLY TO MSG# 3701 (PUBLIC DATA NET)
Primenet is a loal area network.  I know of one in Poole, And BTGold use one
between their systems too. It is only an internal network, I suggest using PSS
to communicate between diffferent primes.  Cheers.

<N>ext msg, <R>eply, or <S>top?

Msg#: 3799 *BBC*
02/07/84 22:09:05 (Read 4 Times)
From: xxxxx xxxxxxx
To: xxxxx xxxxxxx
Subj: REPLY TO MSG# 3751 (RGB VIDEO)
The normal video output BNC can be made to produce colour video by making a
link near to the bnc socket on the pcb. details are in the advanced user guide
under the chapter on what the various links do. If you require more I will try
to help, as I have done this mod and it works fine

Msg#:  935 *EREWHON*
09/20/83 01:23:00 (Read 90 Times)
From: xxxxx xxxx
To: ALL
Subj: US PHONE FREAKING
USA Phone Freaking is done with a 2 out of 5 Code.   The tones must be with 30
Hz, and have less than 1 % Distortion.

Master Tone Frequency = 2600 Hz.
>1 = 700 & 900 Hz
>2 = 700 & 1100 Hz
>3 = 900 & 1100 Hz
>4 = 700 & 1300 Hz
>5 = 900 & 1300 Hz
>6 = 1100 & 1300 Hz
>7 = 700 & 1500 Hz
>8 = 900 & 1500 Hz
>9 ? 1100 & 1500 Hz
>0 = 1300 & 1500 Hz
>Start Key Signal = 1100 & 1700 Hz
>End Key Signal = 1300 & 1700 Hz
> Military Priority Keys 11=700 & 1700 ; 12=900 & 1700 - I don't reccomend
using these. (
The method of use will be explained in a separate note. DO NOT DISCLOSE WHERE
YOU GOT THESE FREQUENCIES TO ANYONE!


Msg#:  936 *EREWHON*
09/20/83 01:34:43 (Read 89 Times)
From: xxxxx xxxx
To: ALL
Subj: UK PHONE FREAKING

The UK system also uses a 2 out of 5 tone pattern.

The Master Frequency is 2280 Hz
>1 = 1380 & 1500 Hz
>2 = 1380 & 1620 Hz
>3 = 1500 & 1620 Hz
>4 = 1380 & 1740 Hz
>5 = 1500 & 1740 Hz
>6 = 1620 & 1740 Hz
>7 = 1380 & 1860 Hz
>8 = 1500 & 1860 Hz
>9 = 1620 & 1860 Hz
>0 = 1740 & 1860 Hz
>Start Key = 1740 & 1980 ; End Keying = .1860 & 1980 Hz
>Unused I think 11 = 1380 & 1980 ; 12 = 1500 & 1980 Hz

This is from the CCITT White Book Vol. 6 and is known as SSMF No. 3 to some
B.T. Personnel.


The 2280 Hz tone is being filtered out at many exchanges so you may need quite
a high level for it to work.

Msg#: 951 *EREWHON*
09/21/83 17:44:28 (Read 79 Times)
From: xxxxxxxxxxx
To: PHONE FREAKS
Subj: NEED YOU ASK ?

In two other messages you will find the frequencies listed for the internal
phone system controls. This note is intended to explain how the system could be
operated. The central feature to realise is that ( expecially in the USA) the
routing information in a call is not in the Dialled Code. The normal sequence
of a call is that the Area Code is received while the Subscriber No. is stored
for a short period. The Local Exchange reads the area code and selects 4he best
route at that time for the call.    The call together with a new "INTERNAThe
call together with a new "INTERNAL" dialling code is then sent on to the next
exchange together with the subscriber number. This is repeated from area to
area and group to group.    The system this way provides many routes and corrects
itself for failures.

The Technique.    Make a Long Distance call to a number which does not answer.
Send down the Master Tone. (2600 or 22080 Hz) This will clear the line back,
but leave you in the system. You may now send the "Start Key Pulse" followed by
the Routing Code and the Subscriber No. Finish with the "End Keying Pulse". The
system sees you as being a distant exchange requesting a route for a call.

Meanwhile back at the home base.    Your local exchange will be logging you in as
still ringing on the first call. There are further problems in this in both the
USA and the UK as the techniques are understood and disapproved of by those in
authority. You may need to have a fairly strong signal into the system to get
past filters present on the line. Warning newer exchanges may link these
filters to alarms.    Try from a phone box or a Public Place and see what happens
or who comes.

Example:- To call from within USA to UK:-
> Ring Toll Free 800 Number
> Send 2600 Hz Key Pulse
> When line goes dead you are in trunk level
> Start Pulse 182 End Pulse = White Plains N.Y. Gateway continued in next
message


Msg#: 952 *EREWHON*
09/21/83 18:03:12 (Read 73 Times)
From: xxxxxxxxxxx
To: PHONE FREAKS
Subj: HOW TO DO IT PT 2

> Start Pulse 044  = United Kingdom
> 1 = Londof ( Note no leading 0 please )
> 730 1234 = Harrods Department Store.

Any info on internal address codes would be appreciated from any callers.


Msg#: 1028 *EREWHON*
09/25/83 23:02:35 (Read 94 Times)
From: xxxx xxxxxxxx
To: ALL
Subj: FREEFONE PART 1


The following info comes from a leaflet entitled 'FREEFONE':

"British Telecom's recent record profits and continuing appalling service have
prompted the circulation of this information. It comprises a method of making
telephone calls free of charge."
.pa
Circuit Diagram:

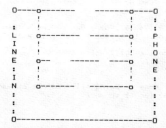

46

```
S1 = 
C1 = 
D1 = 
D2 = 
R1 = 
```

continued...

Circuit Operation:

The circuit inhibits the charging for incoming calls only. When a phone is
answered, there is normally approx. 100mA DC loop current but only 8mA or so is
necessary to polarise the mic In the handset. Drawing only this small amount is
sufficient to fool BT's ancient 'Electric Meccano'.

It's extremely simple. When ringing, the polarity of the line reverses so D1
effectively answers the call when the handset is lifted. When the call is
established, the line polarity reverts and R1 limits the loop current while D2
is a LED to indicate the circuit is in operation. C1 ensures speECh is
unaffected. S1 returns the telephone to normal.

Local calls of unlimited length can be made free of charge. Long disTance calls
using this circuit are prone to automatic disconnection, this varies from area
to area but you will get at least 3 minutes before the line is closed down.
Further experimentation should bear fruit in this respect.

Sith the phone on the hook this circuit is completely undetectable. The swItch
should be cLosed if a call iS received from an operator, for example, or to
make an outgoing call. It has proved extremely useful, particularly for friends
phoning from payphones with jammed coin slots.

*Please DO NOT tell ANYONE where yoU found this information*

Free Test Numbers
=================
Here are some no's that have been found to work:
Dial 174 <last 4 figs of your no>: this gives unobtainable then when you
replace handset the phone rings.
Dial 175 <last 4 figs of your no>: this gives 'start test...start test...',
then when you hang-up the phone rings. Pick it up and you either get dial tone
whiah indicates OK or you will get a recording i.e 'poor insulation B line'
telLing you what's wrong. If you get dial tone you can immediately dial 1305 to
do a further test which might say 'faulty dial pulses'.
Other numbers to try are 182, 184 or 185.
I have discovered my exchange (Pontybodkin) gives a test ring for 1267.
These numbers all depend on you local exchange so It pays to experiment, try
numbers starting with 1 aS thEse are all local functIons. Then when you
discover something of interest let me know on this SIG.

There is a company (?) in the USA called Loopmaniacs Unlimited , PO Box 1197,
Port Townsend, WA, 98368, who publish a line of books on telephone hacking.
Some have circuits even.   Write to M. Hoy there.

One of their publcns is "Steal This Book" at $5.95 plus about $4 post.  Its
worth stealing, but don't show it to the customs!

Msg#: 3266 *EREWHON*
01/22/84 06:25:01 (Read 53 Times)
From: xxx xxxxxxx
To: ALL
Subj: UNIVERSITY COMPUTERS
As already described getting onto the UCL PAD allows various calls. Via this
network you can access many many university/research ck]]~puters To get a full
list use CALL 40 then HELP, select GUIDE. Typing '32' at the VIEW prompt will
start listing the addresses. Most of these can be used at the pad by 'CALL
addr' where addr is the address. For passwords yotry DEMO, HELP etc. If you
find anything interesting report it here.
HINT: To aviod the PAD hanging up at the end of each call use the LOGON command
- use anything for name and pwd. This seems to do the trick.
Another number: Tel: (0235) 834531. This is another data exchange. This one's a
bit harder to wake up. You must send a 'break level' to start. This can be done
using software but with a maplin just momentarily pull out the RS232 conn. Then
send RETURNs. To get a list od 'classes' you could use say Manchesters HELP:-
CALL 1020300, user:DEMO pwd:DEMO en when you're on HELP PACX.


Msg#: 3687 *HACKER'S CLUB*
02/05/84 14:41:43 (Read 416 Times)
From: xxxx xxxxxxx
To: ALL
Subj: HACKERS NUMBERS

The following are some of the numbers collected in the Hackers SIG:
*********
Commodore BBS (Finland)        358 61 116223
*********
Gateway test                   01 600 1261
PRESTEST (1200/75)             01 583 9412
Some  usaful PRESTEL nodes - 640..Res.D (Martlesham's experiments
in  Dynamic Prestel,  DRCS, CEPT standards, Picture Prestel), 601
(Mailbox,Telemessaging,  Telex Link - and maybe  Telecom  Gold),
651 (Scratchpad -always changing).  Occasionally parts of 650 (IP
News)  are not properly CUGed off.  190 sometimes is  interesting
as well.
*********
These boards all specialise in lonely hearts services !
The boards with an asterisk all use BELL Tones
*Fairbanks, AK, 907-479-0315
*Burbank, CA,   213-840-8252
*Burbank, CA,   213-842-9452
*Clovis, CA,    209-298-1328
*Glendale, CA,  213-242-1882
*La Palma, CA   714-220-0239
*Hollywood, CA, 213-764-8000
*San Francisco CA 415-467-2588
*Santa Monica CA, 213-390-3239
*Sherman Oaks CA, 213-990-6830
*Tarzana , CA,    213-345-1047
*Crystal River, FL904-795-8850
*Atlanta, GA,      912-233-0863
*Hammond, IN,     219-845-4200
*Cleveland, OH,   216-932-9845
*Lynnefield, MA,  617-334-6369
*Omaha, NE,       402-571-8942
*Freehold, NJ,    201-462-0435
*New York, NY,    212-541-5975
*Cary, NC,        919-362-0676
*Newport News,VA  804-838-3973
*Vancouver, WA,   206-256-6624
Marseilles, France 33-91-91-0660
*********
Both USA nos. prefix (0101)
a) Daily X-rated Joke Service 516-922-9463
b)  Auto-Biographies of  young  ladies  who  normally  work   in
unpublishable magazines on 212-976-2727.
c)Dial a w**K; 0101,212,976,2626; 0101,212,976,2727;

  Msg#: 3688 *HACKER'S CLUB*
  02/05/84 14:44:51 (Read 393 Times)
  From: xxxx xxxxxxx
  To: ALL
  Subj: HACKERS NUMBERS CONT...

48

Hertford  PDP 11/70 Hackers BBS:
Call 0707-263577 with 110 baud selected.
type: SET SPEED 300<CR>
After hitting CR switch to 300 baud.
Then type: HELLO 124,4<CR>
!Password: HAE4<CR>
When logged on type: COMMAND HACKER<CR>
Use: BYE to log out.
*********
EUCLID              388-2333
TYPE A COUPLE OF <CR> THEN PAD <CR>
ONCE LOGGED ON TO PAD TYPE CALL 40  <CR>  TRY DEMO AS A USERID  WHY NOT
TRY A FEW DIFFRER DIFFERENT CALLS  THIS WILL LET U LOG ON TO A WHOLE
NETWORK SYSTEM ALL OVER EUROPE!
YOU CAN ALSO USE 01-278-4355.
*********
Unknown 300 Baud        01-854 2411
01-854 2499
*********
Honeywell:From London dial the 75, else 0753(SLOUGH)
75 74199 75 76930
Type: TSS
User id: DD1003
password: Unwnown (up to 10 chars long)
Type: EXPL GAMES LIST to list gamec
To run a game type: FRN GAMES/(NAME),E for a fortran game.
Replace FRN with BRN for BASIC games.
*********
Central London Poly     01 637 7732/3/4/5
*********
PSS (300)               0753 6141
*********
Comshare (300)          01 351 2311
*********
'Money Box'             01 828 9090
*********
Imperial College        01 581 1366
01 581 1444
*********
These are most of the interesting numbers that have come up over the
last bit. If I have omitted any, please leave them in a message.

Cheers, xxxx.


Msg#: 5156 *HACKER'S CLUB*
04/15/84 08:01:11 (Read 221 Times)
From: xxxxx xxxxxx
To: ALL
Subj: FINANCIAL DATABASES
You can get into Datastream on dial-up at 300/300 on 251 6180 -
no I don't have any passwords....you can get into Inter Company
Comparisons (ICC) company database of 60,000 companies via their
1200/75 viewdata front-end processor on 253 8788. Type **** when
asked for your company  code to see a demo...


Msg#: 5195 *HACKER'S CLUB*
04/17/84 02:28:10 (Read 229 Times)
From: xxxxxxxx xxxxxxx
To: ALL
Subj: PSS TELEX
THIS IS PROBOBLY OLD HAT BY NOW BUT IF YOU USE PSS THEN A92348****** WHERE
**=UK TELEX NO. USE CTRL/P CLR TO GET OUT AFTER MESSAGE. YOU WILL BE CHARGED
FOR USE I GESS.


Msg#: 7468 *EREWHON*
06/29/84 23:30:24 (Read 27 Times)
From: xxxxxx xxxxxx
To: PHREAKS
Subj: NEW(OLD..) INFO
TODAY I WAS LUCKY ENOUGH TO DISCOVER A PREVIOUSLY UNKNOWN CACHE OF THE AMERICAN
MAGAZINE KNOWN AS TAP. ALTHO THEYRE RATHER OUT OF DATE (1974-1981) OR SO THEY
ARE PRETTY FUNNY AND HAVE A FEW  INTERESTING BITS OF INFORMATION, ESPECIALLY IF

49

U WANT TO SEE THE CIRCUIT DIAGRAMS OF UNTOLD AMOUNTS OF BLUE/RED/BLACK/???
BOXES THERE ARE EVEN A FEW SECTIONS ON THE UK (BUT AS I SAID ITS COMPLETELY
OUT OF DATE). IN THE FUTURE I WILL POST SOME OF THE GOOD STUFF FROM TAP ON
THIS BOARD (WHEN AND IF I CAN GET ON THIS BLOODY SYSTEM!!). ALSO I MANAGED TO
FIND A HUGE BOOK PUBLISHED BY AT&T ON DISTANCE DIALING (DATED 1975). DUNNO, IF
ANYBODY'S INTERESTED THEN LEAVE A NOTE REQUESTING ANY INFO YOU'RE AFTER CHEERS
PS ANYBODY KNOW DEPRAVO THE RAT?? DOES HE STILL LIVE?


Msg#: 7852 *HACKER'S CLUB*
08/17/84 00:39:05 (Read 93 Times)
From: xxxx xxxxx
To: ALL USERS
Subj: NKABBS
NKABBS IS NOW ONLINE. FOR ATARI & OTHER MICRO USERS. OPERATING ON 300 BAUD VIA
RINGBACK SYSTEM. TIMES 2130HRS-2400HRS DAILY. TEL :0795 842324. SYSTEM UP AT
THESE TIMES ONLY UNTIL RESPONSE GROWS. ALL USERS ARE WELCOME TO LOGON.
EVENTUALLY WE WILL BE SERVING BBC,COMMDORE VIC 20/64 OWNERS.+NEWS ETC.

Msg#:8154 *EREWHON*
08/02/84 21:46:11 (Read 13 Times)
From: ANON
To: ALL
Subj: REPLY TO MSG# !1150 (PHREAK BOARDS)


[][][][][][][][][][][][][][]
[] PHREAK BOARD NUMBERS []
[]     ACROSS THE U.S.    []
[][][][][][][][][][][][][][]

IF YOU KNOW OF A BOARD THAT IS NOT LISTED HERE, PLEASE LET ME KNOW ABOUT IT.

| | | | |
|---|---|---|---|
| JOLLY ROGER | 713-468-0174 | PIRATE'S BEACH | 305-865-5432 |
| PIRATE'S CHEST | 617-981-1349 | PIRATE'S COVE | 516-698-4008 |
| PIRATE'S DATA CENTER | 213-341-3962 | PIRATE'S WAREHOUSE | 415-924-8338 |
| PIRATE'S SPACE STATION | 617-244-8244 | PIRATE'S PORT | 512-345-3752 |
| PIRATE'S OUTHOUSE | 301-299-3953 | PIRATE'S NEWSTAND ][ | 213-373-3318 |
| PIRATE'S HANDLE ][ | 314-434-6187 | PIRATE'S GOLDMINE | 617-443-7428 |
| PIRATE'S DREAM | 713-997-5067 | PIRATE'S SHIP | 312-445-3883 |
| PIRATE'S TRADE | 213-932-8294 | PIRATE'S MOUNTAIN | 213-472-4287 |
| PIRATE'S TREK | 914-634-1268 | PIRATE'S TREK ][ | 914-967-2917 |
| PIRATE'S TREK III | 914-835-3627 | PIRATE'S TREK IV | 714-932-1124 |
| PIRATE-80 | 305-225-8059 | PORT OR THIEVES | 305-798-1051 |
| SANCTUARY | 201-891-9567 | SECRET SERVICE | 213-932-8294 |
| SECRET SERVICE ][ | 215-855-7913 | SHERWOOD FOREST | 212-896-6063 |
| SKELETON ISLAND | 804-285-0041 | GALAXY ONE | 215-224-0864 |
| BOCA HARBOR | 305-392-5924 | R.A.G.T.I.M.E. | 217-429-6310 |
| PIRATES OF PUGET SOUND | 206-783-9798 | KINGDOM OF SEVEN | 206-767-7777 |
| THE INSANITARIUM | 609-234-6106 | THE STAR SYSTEM | 516-698-7345 |
| HAUNTED MANSION | 516-367-8172 | ALPHANET | 203-227-2987 |
| WASTELANDS | 513-761-8250 | HACKER HEAVEN | 516-796-6454 |
| PIRATE'S HARBOR | 617-720-3600 | PHANTOM ACCESS | 814-868-1884 |
| SKULL ISLAND | 203-972-1685 | THE CONNECTION | 516-487-1774 |
| THE TEMPLE | 305-798-1615 | THE TAVERN | 516-623-9004 |
| SIR LANCELOT'S CASTLE | 914-381-2124 | PIRATE'S HIDEAWAY | 617-449-2808 |
| PIRATE'S CITY | 703-780-0610 | PIRATE'S PILLAGE | 317-743-5789 |
| PIRATE'S GALLEY | 213-796-6602 | THE PARADISE ON-LINE | 512-477-2672 |
| THE PAWN SHOPPE | 213-859-2735 | MAD BOARD FROM MARS | 213-470-5912 |
| MISSION CONTROL | 301-983-8293 | NERVOUS SYSTEM | 305-554-9332 |
| BIG BLUE MONSTER | 305-781-1683 | DEVO | 305-652-9422 |
| THE I.C.'S SOCKET | 213-541-5607 | TORTURE CHAMBER | 213-375-6137 |
| THE MAGIC REALM | 212-767-9046 | HELL | 914-835-4919 |
| PIRATE'S BAY | 415-775-2384 | CRASHER BBS | 415-461-8215 |
| BEYOND BELIEF | 213-377-6568 | ALCATRAZ | 301-881-0846 |
| PIRATE'S TROVE | 703-644-1665 | THE TRADING POST | 504-291-4970 |
| CHEYANNE MOUNTAIN | 303-753-1554 | DEATH STAR | 312-627-5138 |
| ALAMO CITY | 512-623-6123 | THE CPU | 313-547-7903 |
| CROWS NEST | 617-862-7037 | TRADER'S INN | 618-856-3321 |
| PIRATE'S PUB ][ | 617-891-5793 | PIRATE'S PUB | 617-894-7266 |
| PIRATE'S I/O | 201-543-6139 | BLUEBEARDS GALLEY | 213-842-0227 |
| SOUNDCHASER | 804-788-0774 | MIDDLE EARTH | 213-334-4323 |
| SPLIT INFINITY | 408-867-4455 | EXIDY 2000 | 713-442-7644 |
| CAPTAIN'S LOG | 612-377-7747 | SHERWOOD FOREST ][ | 914-352-6543 |
| THE SILMARILLION ][ | 714-535-7527 | WARLOCK'S CASTLE | 618-345-6638 |
| TWILIGHT PHONE | 313-775-1649 | TRON | 312-675-1819 |

| THE UNDERGROUND | 707-996-2427 | THE SAFEHOUSE | 612-724-7066 |
|---|---|---|---|
| THE INTERFACE | 213-477-4605 | THE GRAPE VINE | 612-454-6209 |
| THE DOC BOARD | 713-471-4131 | THE ARK | 701-343-6426 |
| SYSTEM SEVEN | 415-232-7200 | SPACE VOYAGE | 713-530-5249 |
| SHADOW WORLD | 713-777-8608 | OXGATE | 804-898-7493 |
| OUTER LIMITS | 213-784-0204 | MINES OF MORIA ][ | 408-688-9629 |
| METRO | 313-855-6321 | MERLIN'S TOWER | 914-381-2374 |
| MAGUS | 703-471-0611 | GREENTREE | 919-282-4205 |
| GHOST SHIP III - PENTAGON | 312-627-5138 | GHOST SHIP ][ - ARAGORNS | 312-644-5165 |
| GHOST SHIP - TARDIS | 312-528-1611 | GENERAL HOSPITAL | 201-992-9893 |
| DATA THIEVES | 312-392-2403 | DARK REALM | 713-333-2309 |
| DANGER ISLAND | 409-846-2900 | COSMIC VOYAGE | 713-530-5249 |
| CORRUPT COMPUTING | 313-453-9183 | CAMELOT | 312-357-8075 |
| THE ORACLE | 305-475-9062 | PIRATE'S GUILD | 312-279-4399 |
| PIRATE'S PLANET | 901-756-0026 | HKGES | 305-676-5312 |
| CAESER'S PALACE | 305-253-9869 | MINES OF MORIA | 713-871-8577 |
| CRASHER BBS | 415-461-8215 | A.S.C.I.I. | 301-984-3772 |

If anybody is mad enough to actually dial up one (or more!) of these BBs please
log everything so that others may benefit from your efforts. IE- WE only have
to register once, and we find out if this board suits our interest. Good luck
and have fun! Cheers,

Msg#: 8163 *HACKER'S CLUB*
08/30/84 18:55:27 (Read 78 Times)
From: xxxxxxxx xxxxxxx
To: ALL
Subj: ****************************
NBBS East is a relatively new bulletin board running from 10pm to 1230am on
0692 630610. There are now special facilties for BBC users with colour,
graphics etc. If you call it then please try to leave some messages as more
messages mean more callers, which in turn means more messages Thanks a lot, Jon

Msg#: 8601 *HACKER'S CLUB*
09/17/84 10:52:43 (Read 57 Times)
From: xxxx xxxxxxx
To: xxxx xxxxxxx
Subj: REPLY TO MSG# 8563 (HONEYWELL)
The thing is I still ( sort of ) work for XXX so I don't think they would be
too pleased if I gave out numbers or anything else, and I would rather keepmy
job. Surely you don't mean MFI furniture ??

Msg#: 8683 *HACKER'S CLUB*
09/19/84 19:54:05 (Read 63 Times)
From: xxxxx xxxxxxxxxx
To: ALL
Subj: DATA NODE
To those who have difficulty finding interesting numbers, try the UCL Data Node
on 01-388 2333    (300 baud).When you get the Which Service? prompt, type PAD
and a couple of CRs. Then, when the PAD>
prompt appears type CALL X00X00X, where is any(number orrange of numbers.
Indeed, you can try several formats and numbers until you find something
interesting. The Merlin Cern computer is 9002003. And it's difficult to trace
you through a data exchange! If anyone finds any interesting numbers, let me
know on this board, or Pretzel mailbox 012495225.

Msg has replies, read now(Y/N)? Y

Msg#: 9457 *HACKER'S CLUB*
10/11/84 01:52:56 (Read 15 Times)
From: xxxxxx xxxxxxxxxx
To: xxxxx xxxxxxxxx
Subj: REPLY TO MSG# 8683 (DATA NODE)
IF YOU WANT TO KNOW MORE ABOUT THIS xxxxx PHIN PHONE xxxx xxxxxx
ON 000 0000

Msg#: 8785 *HACKER'S CLUB*
09/21/84 20:28:59 (Read 40 Times)
From: xxxx xxxxS
To: ALL
Subj: NEW NUMBER
NEW COMPUTER ON LINE TRY RINGING 960 7868 SORRY THATS 01 (IN LONDON) IN FRONT.
GOOD LUCK!

Please note that none of these hints, rumours, phone numbers and passwords are likely to work by the time you are reading this... However, in the case of the US credit agency TRW, described in the previous chapter, valid phone numbers and passwords appear to have sat openly on a number of bulletin boards for up to a year before the agency realised it. Some university mainframes have hacker's boards hidden on them as well.

It is probably bad taste to mention it, but of course people try to hack bulletin boards as well. An early version of one of the most popular packages could be hacked simply by sending two semi-colons (;;) when asked for your name. The system allowed you to become the Sysop, even though you were sitting at a different computer; you could access the user file, complete with all passwords, validate or devalidate whomever you liked, destroy mail, write general notices, and create whole new areas...

**Research Sources**
The computer industry has found it necessary to spend vast sums on marketing its products and whilst some of that effort is devoted to 'image' and 'concept' type advertising — to making senior management comfortable with the idea of the XXX Corporation's hardware because it has 'heard' of it — much more is in the form of detailed product information.

This information surfaces in glossies, in conference papers, and in magazine journalism. Most professional computer magazines are given away on subscription to 'qualified' readers; mostly the publisher wants to know if the reader is in a position to influence a key buying decision — or is looking for a job.

I have never had any difficulty in being regarded as qualified: certainly no one ever called round to my address to check up the size of my mainframe installation or the number of employees. If in doubt, you can always call yourself a consultant. Registration is usually a matter of filling in a post-paid card. My experience is that, once you are on a few subscription lists, more magazines, unasked for, tend to arrive every week or month — together with invitations to expensive conferences in far-off climes. Do not be put off by the notion that free magazines must be garbage. In the computer industry, as in the medical world, this is absolutely not the case. Essential regular reading for hackers are *Computing, Computer Weekly, Software, Datalink, Communicate, Communications Management, Datamation, Mini-Micro Systems*, and *Telecommunications*.

The articles and news items often contain information of use to hackers: who is installing what, where; what sort of facilities are being offered; what new products are appearing and what features they have. Sometimes you will find surveys of sub-sets of the computer industry. Leafing through the magazine pile that has accumulated while this chapter was being written, I have marked for special attention a feature on Basys Newsfury, an electronic newsroom package used, among others, by ITN's Channel Four News; several articles on new on-line hosts; an explanation of new enhanced Reuters services; a comparison of various private viewdata software packages and who is using them; some puffs for new Valued Added Networks (VANs); several pieces on computer security; news of credit agencies selling on-line and via viewdata; and a series on Defence Data Networks.

In most magazines, however, this is not all: each advertisement is coded with a number which you have to circle on a tear-out post-paid 'bingo card': each one you mark will bring wads of useful information: be careful, however, to give just enough information about yourself to ensure that postal packets arrive and not sufficient to give the 'I was just passing in the neighbourhood and thought I would call in to see if I could help' sales rep a 'lead' he thinks he can exploit.

Another excellent source of information are exhibitions: there are the ubiquitous 'product information' sheets, but also the actual machines and software to look at and maybe play with; perhaps you can even get a full scale demonstration and interject a few questions. The real bonus of exhibitions, of course, is that the security sense of salespersons, exhausted by performing on a stand for several days and by the almost compulsory off-hours entertainment of top clients or attempted seduction of the hired-in 'glamour' is rather low. Passwords are often written down on paper and consulted in your full view. All you need is a quick eye and a reasonable memory.

At both exhibitions and conferences it is a good idea to be a freelance journalist. Most computer mags have relatively small full-time staff and rely on freelancers, so you won't be thought odd. And you'll have your questions answered without anyone asking 'And how soon do you think you'll be making a decision?'

Sometimes the lack of security at exhibitions and demonstrations defies belief. When ICL launched its joint venture product with Sinclair, the One-Per-Desk communicating executive workstations, it embarked on a modest road-show to give hands-on experience to prospective purchasers. The demonstration models had been pre-loaded with phone numbers...of senior ICL directors, of the ICL mainframe at its headquarters in Putney and various other remote services....

Beyond these open sources of information are a few murkier ones. The most important aid in tackling a 'difficult' operating system or applications program is the proper documentation: this can be obtained in a variety of ways. Sometimes a salesman may let you look at a manual while you 'help' him find the bit of information he can't remember from his sales training. Perhaps an employee can provide a 'spare', or run you a photocopy. In some cases, you may even find the manual stored electronically on the system; in which case, print it out. Another desirable document is an organisation's internal phone book...it may give you the numbers for the computer ports, but failing that, you will be able to see the *range* of numbers in use and, if you are using an auto-dial modem coupled with a search-and-try program, you will be able to define the search parameters more carefully. A phone book will also reveal the names of computer managers and system engineers; perhaps they use fairly obvious passwords.

It never ceases to astonish me what organisations leave in refuse piles without first giving them a session with the paper shredder.

I keep my cuttings carefully stored away in a second-hand filing cabinet; items that apply to more than one interest area are duplicated in the photocopier.

## Inference

But hackers' research doesn't rely simply on collecting vast quantities of paper against a possible use. If you decide to target on a particular computer or network, it is surprising what can be found out with just a little effort. Does the organisation that owns the system publish any information about it. In a handbook, annual report, house magazine? When was the hardware and software installed? Did any of the professional weekly computer mags write it up? What do you know about the hardware, what sorts of operating systems would you expect to see, who supplied the software, do you know anyone with experience of similar systems, and so on.

By way of illustration, I will describe certain inferences it is reasonable to make about the principal installation used by Britain's Security Service, MI5. At the end, you will draw two conclusions: first that someone seriously interested in illicitly extracting information from the computer would find the traditional techniques of espionage — suborning of MI5 employees by bribery, blackmail or appeal to ideology — infinitely easier than pure hacking; and second, that remarkable detail can be accumulated about machines and systems, the very existence of which is supposed to be a secret — and by using purely open sources and reasonable guess-work.

The MI5 databanks and associated networks have long been the subject of interest to civil libertarians. Few people would deny absolutely the need for an internal security service of some sort, nor deny that service the benefit of the latest technology. But, civil libertarians ask, who are the legitimate targets of MI5's activities? If they are 'subversives', how do you define them? By looking at the type of computer power MI5 and its associates possess, it possible to see if perhaps they are casting too wide a net for anyone's good. If, as has been suggested, the main installation can hold and access 20 million records, each containing 150 words, and Britain's total population including children, is 56 million, then perhaps an awful lot of individuals are being marked as 'potential subversives'.

It was to test these ideas out that two journalists, not themselves out-and-out hackers, researched the evidence upon which hackers have later built. The two writers were Duncan Campbell of the *New Statesman* and Steve Connor, first of *Computing* and more recently on the *New Scientist*. The inferences work this way: the only computer manufacturer likely to be entrusted to supply so sensitive a customer would be British and the single candidate would be ICL. You must therefore look at their product range and decide which items would be suitable for a really large, secure, real-time database management job. In the late 1970s, the obvious path was the 2900 series, possibly doubled up and with substantive rapid-access disc stores of the type EDS200.

Checking through back issues of trade papers it is possible to see that just such a configuration, in fact a dual 2980 with a 2960 as back-up and 20 gigabytes of disc store, were ordered for classified database work by 'the Ministry of Defence'. ICL, on questioning by the journalists, confirmed that they had sold 3 such large systems, two abroad and one for a UK government department. Campbell and Connor were able to establish the site of the computer, in Mount Row, London W1, and, in later stories, gave more detail, this time obtained by a careful study of advertisements placed by two recruitment agencies over several years. The main computer, for example, has several minis attached to it, and at least 200 terminals. The journalists later went on to investigate details of the networks — connections between National Insurance, Department of Health, police and vehicle driving license systems.

In fact, at a technical level, and still keeping to open sources, you can build up even more detailed speculations about the MI5 main computer. ICL's communication protocols, CO1, CO2, CO3, are published items; you can get terminal emulators to work on a PC, and both the company and its employees have published accounts of their approaches to database management systems, which, incidentally, integrate software and hardware functions to an unusually high degree, giving speed but also a great deal of security at fundamental operating system level.

Researching MI5 is an extreme example of what is possible; there are few computer installations of which it is in the least difficult to assemble an almost complete picture.

# CHAPTER 6

# Hackers' Techniques

The time has now come to sit at the keyboard, phone and modems at the ready, relevant research materials convenient to hand and see what you can access. In keeping with the 'handbook' nature of this publication, I have put my most solid advice in the form of a trouble-shooting appendix (I), so this chapter talks around the techniques rather than spelling them out in great detail.

**Hunting instincts**
Good hacking, like birdwatching and many other pursuits, depends ultimately on raising your intellectual knowledge almost to instinctive levels. The novice twitcher will, on being told 'There's a kingfisher!', roam all over the skies looking for the little bird and probably miss it. The experienced ornithologist will immediately look low over a patch of water, possibly a section shaded by trees, because kingfishers are known to gulp the sort of flies that hover over streams and ponds. Similarly, a good deal of skilful hacking depends on knowing what to expect and how to react. The instinct takes time to grow, but the first step is understanding that you need to develop it in the first place.

**Tricks with phones**
If you don't have a complete phone number for a target computer, then you can get an auto-dialler and a little utility program to locate it for you. You will find a flow-chart for a program in Appendix VII. An examination of the phone numbers in the vicinity of the target machine should give you a range within which to search. The program then accesses the auto-dial mechanism of the modem and 'listens' for any whistles. The program should enable the phone line to be disconnected after two or three 'rings' as auto-answer modems have usually picked up by then.

Such programs and their associated hardware are a little more complicated than the popularised portrayals suggest: you must have software to run sequences of calls through your auto-dialler, the hardware must tell you whether you have scored a 'hit' with a modem or merely dialled a human being, and, since the whole point of the exercise is that it works unattended, the process must generate a list of numbers to try.

**Logging on**

You dial up, hear a whistle...and the VDU stays blank. What's gone wrong? Assuming your equipment is not at fault, the answer must lie either in wrong speed setting or wrong assumed protocol. Experienced hackers listen to a whistle from an unknown computer before throwing the data button on the modem or plunging the phone handset into the rubber cups of an acoustic coupler. Different tones indicate different speeds and the trained ear can easily detect the difference — appendix III gives the common variants.

Some modems, particularly those on mainframes, can operate at more than one speed; the user sets it by sending the appropriate number of carriage returns. In a typical situation, the mainframe answers at 110 baud (for teletypewriters), and two carriage returns take it up to 300 baud, the normal default for asynchronous working.

Some hosts will not respond until they receive a character from the user. Try sending a space or a carriage return.

If these obvious things don't work and you continue to get no response, try altering the protocol settings (see chapters 2 and 3). Straightforward asynchronous protocols with 7-bit ASCII, odd or even parity and surrounded by one stop and one start bit is the norm, but almost any variant is possible.

Once you start getting a stream from the host, you must evaluate it to work out what to do next. Are all the lines over-writing each other and not scrolling down the screen? Get your terminal software to insert carriage returns. Are you getting a lot of corruption? Check your phone connections and your protocols. The more familiar you are with your terminal software at this point, the more rapidly you will get results.

**Passwords**

Everyone thinks they know how to invent plausible and acceptable passwords; here are the ones that seem to come up over and over again:

HELP • TEST • TESTER • SYSTEM • SYSTEM
MANAGER • SYSMAN • SYSOP • ENGINEER •
OPS • OPERATIONS • CENTRAL • DEMO •
DEMONSTRATION • AID • DISPLAY • CALL •
TERMINAL • EXTERNAL • REMOTE • CHECK •
NET • NETWORK • PHONE • FRED

Are you puzzled by the special inclusion of FRED? Look at your computer keyboard sometime and see how easily the one-fingered typist can find those four letters!

If you know of individuals likely to have legitimate access to a system, find out what you can about them to see if you can second-guess their choice of personal password. Own names, or those of loved ones, or initials are the top favourites. Sometimes there is some slight anagramming and other forms of obvious jumbling. If the password is numeric, the obvious things to try are birthdays, home phone numbers, vehicle numbers, bank account numbers (as displayed on cheques) and so on.

Sometimes numeric passwords are even easier to guess: I have found myself system manager of a private viewdata system simply by offering it the password 1234567890 and other hackers have been astonished at the results obtained from 11111111, 22222222 etc or 1010101, 2020202.

It is a good idea to see if you can work on the mentality and known pre-occupations of the legitimate password holder: if he's keen on classic rock n'roll, you could try ELVIS; a gardener might choose CLEMATIS; Tolkien readers almost invariably select FRODO or BILBO; those who read Greek and Roman Literature at ancient universities often assume that no one would ever guess a password like EURIPIDES; it is a definitive rule that radio amateurs never use anything other than their call-signs.

Military users like words like FEARLESS and VALIANT or TOPDOG; universities, large companies and public corporations whose various departments are known by acronyms (like the BBC) can find those initials reappearing as passwords.

One less-publicised trick is to track down the name of the top person in the organisation and guess a computer identity for them; the hypothesis is that they were invited to try the computer when it was first opened and were given an 'easy' password which has neither been used since nor wiped from the user files. A related trick is to identify passwords associated with the hardware or software installer; usually the first job of a system manager on taking over a computer is to remove such IDs, but often they neglect to do so. Alternatively, a service engineer may have a permanent ID so that, if the system falls over, it can be returned to full activity with the minimum delay.

Nowadays there is little difficulty in devising theoretically secure password systems, and bolstering them by allowing each user only three false attempts before the disconnecting the line, as Prestel does, for example. The real difficulty lies in getting humans to follow the appropriate procedures. Most of us can only hold a limited quantity of character and number sequences reliably in our heads. Make a log-on sequence too complicated, and users will feel compelled to write little notes to themselves, even if expressly forbidden to do so. After a while the complicated process becomes counter-productive. I have a encrypting/decrypting software package for the IBM PC. It is undoubtedly many times more secure than the famous Enigma codes of World War II and after. The trouble is that that you need up to 25 different 14-digit numbers of your specification, which you and your correspondent must share if successful recovery of the original text is to take place.

Unfortunately the most convenient way to store these sequences is in a separate disk file (get one character wrong and decryption is impossible) and it is all too easy to save the key file either with the enciphered stream, or with the software master, in both of which locations they are vulnerable.

Nowadays many ordinary users of remote computer services use terminal emulator software to store their passwords. It is all too easy for the hacker to make a quick copy of a 'proper' user's disk, take it away, and then examine the contents of the various log-on files — usually by going into an 'amend password' option. The way for the legitimate user to obtain protection, other than the obvious one of keeping such disks secure, is to have the terminal software itself password protected, and all files encrypted until the correct password is input. But then that new password has to be committed to the owner's memory....

Passwords can also be embedded in the firmware of a terminal. This is the approach used in many Prestel viewdata sets when the user can, sometimes with the help of the Prestel computer, program his or her set into an EAROM (Electrically Alterable Read Only Memory). If, in the case of Prestel, the entire 14-digit sequence is permanently programmed in the set, that identity (and the user bill associated with it) is vulnerable to the first person who hits the 'viewdata' button on the keypad. Most users only program in the first 10 digits and key in the last four manually. A skilful hacker can make a terminal disgorge its programmed ID by sticking a modem in answer-mode on its back (reversing tones and, in the case of viewdata, speeds also) and sending the ASCII ENQ (ctrl-E) character, which will often cause the user's terminal to send its identity.

A more devious trick with a conventional terminal is to write a little program which overlays the usual sign-on sequence. The program captures the password as it is tapped out by the legitimate user and saves it to a file where the hacker can retrieve it later.

People reuse their passwords. The chances are that, if you

obtain someone's password on one system, the same one will appear on another system to which that individual also has access.

## Programming tricks

In most longish magazine articles about electronic crime, the writer includes a list of 'techniques' with names like Salami, Trap Door and Trojan Horse. Most of these are not applicable to pure hacking, but refer to activities carried out by programmers interested in fraud.

The Salami technique, for example, consists of extracting tiny sums of money from a large number of bank accounts and dumping the proceeds into an account owned by the fraudsman. Typically there's an algorithm which monitors deposits which have as their last digit '8'; it then deducts '1' from that and then £1 or $1 is siphoned off.

The Trojan Horse is a more generalised technique which consists of hiding away a bit of unorthodox active code in a standard legitimate routine. The code could, for example, call a special larger routine under certain conditions and that routine could carry out a rapid fraud before wiping itself out and disappearing from the system for good.

The Trap Door is perhaps the only one of these techniques that pure hackers use. A typical case is when a hacker enters a system with a legitimate identity but is able to access and alter the user files. The hacker than creates a new identity with extra privileges to roam over the system, and is thus able to enter it at any time as a 'super-user' or 'system manager'.

## Hardware tricks

For the hacker with some knowledge of computer hardware and general electronics, and who is prepared to mess about with circuit diagrams, a soldering iron and perhaps a voltmeter, logic probe or oscilloscope, still further possibilities open up. One of the most useful bits of kit consists of a small cheap radio receiver (MW/AM band), a microphone and a tape recorder. Radios in the vicinity of computers, modems and telephone lines can readily pick up the chirp chirp of digital communications without the need of carrying out a physical phone 'tap'.

Alternatively, an inductive loop with a small low-gain amplifier in the vicinity of a telephone or line will give you a recording you can analyse later at your leisure. By identifying the pairs of tones being used, you can separate the caller and the host. By feeding the recorded tones onto an oscilloscope display you can freeze 'bits', 'characters' and 'words'; you can strip off the start and stop bits and, with the aid of an ASCII-to-binary table, examine what is happening. With experience it is entirely possible to identify a wide range of protocols simply from the 'look' of an oscilloscope. A cruder technique is simply to record and playback sign-on sequences; the limitation is that, even if you manage to log on, you may not know what to do afterwards.

Listening on phone lines is of course a technique also used by some sophisticated robbers. In 1982 the Lloyds Bank Holborn branch was raided; the alarm did not ring because the thieves had previously recorded the 'all-clear' signal from the phone line and then, during the break-in, stuffed the recording up the line to the alarm monitoring apparatus.

Sometimes the hacker must devise *ad hoc* bits of hardware trickery in order to achieve his ends. Access has been obtained to a well-known financial prices service largely by stringing together a series of simple hardware skills. The service is available mostly on leased lines, as the normal vagaries of dial-up would be too unreliable for the City folk who are the principal customers. However, each terminal also has an associated dial-up facility, in case the leased line should go down; and in addition, the same terminals can have access to Prestel. Thus the hacker thought that it should be possible to access the service with ordinary viewdata equipment instead of the special units supplied along with the annual subscription. Obtaining the phone number was relatively easy: it was simply a matter of selecting manual dial-up from the appropriate menu, and listening to the pulses as they went through the regular phone.

The next step was to obtain a password. The owners of the terminal to which the hacker had access did not know their ID; they had no need to know it because it was programmed into the terminal and sent automatically. The hacker could have put a micro 'back-to-front' across the line and sent a ENQ to see if an ID would be sent back. Instead he tried something less obvious.

The terminal was known to be programmable, provided one knew how and had the right type of keyboard. Engineers belonging to the service had been seen doing just that. How could the hacker acquire 'engineer' status? He produced the following hypothesis: the keyboard used by the service's customers was a simple affair, lacking many of the obvious keys used by normal terminals; the terminal itself was manufactured by the same company that produced a range of editing terminals for viewdata operators and publishers. Perhaps if one obtained a manual for the editing terminal, important clues might appear. A suitable photocopy was obtained and, lo and behold, there were instructions for altering terminal IDs, setting auto-diallers and so on.

Now to obtain a suitable keyboard. Perhaps a viewdata editing keyboard, or a general purpose ASCII keyboard with switchable baud rates? So far, no hardware difficulties. An examination of the back of the terminal revealed that the supplied keypads used rather unusual connectors, not the 270° 6-pin DIN which is the Prestel standard. The hacker looked in another of his old files and discovered some literature relating to viewdata terminals. Now he knew what sort of things to expect from the strange socket at the back of the special terminal: he pushed in an unterminated plug and proceeded to test the free leads with a volt-meter against what he expected; eight minutes and some cursing later he had it worked out; five minutes after that he had built himself a little patch cord between an ASCII keyboard, set initially to 75 baud and then to 1200 baud as the most likely speeds; one minute later he found the terminal was responding as he had hoped...

Now to see if there were similarities between the programming commands in the equipment for which he had a manual and the equipment he wished to hack. Indeed there were: on the screen before him was the menu and ID and phone data he had hoped to see. The final test was to move over to a conventional Prestel set, dial up the number for the financial service and send the ID.

The hacker himself was remarkably uninterested in the financial world and, after describing to me how he worked his trick, has now gone in search of other targets.

**Operating Systems**

The majority of simple home micros operate only in two modes — Basic or machine code. Nearly all computers of a size greater than this use operating systems which are essentially housekeeping routines, and which tell the processor where to expect instructions from, how to identify and manipulate both active and stored memory, how to keep track of drives and serial ports (and joy-sticks and mice), how to accept data from a keyboard and locate it on a screen, how to dump results to screen or printer or disc drive, and so on. Familiar micro-based operating systems include CP/M, MS-DOS, CP/M-86 and so on, but more advanced operating systems have more facilities — capacity to allow several users all accessing the same data and programs without colliding with each other, enlarged standard utilities to make fast file creation, fast sorting and fast calculation much easier. Under simple operating systems, the programmer has comparatively few tools to help him; often there is just the Basic language, which itself contains no standard procedures — almost everything must be written from scratch each time. But most computer programs rely, in essence, on a small set of standard modules: forms to accept data to a program, files to keep the data in, calculations to transform that data, techniques to sort the data, forms to present the data to the user upon demand, the ability to present results in various graphics, and so on. So programs written under more advanced operating systems tend to be comparatively briefer for the same end-result than those with Basic acting not only as a language, but also as the computer's housekeeper.

When you enter a mainframe computer as an ordinary customer, you will almost certainly be located in an applications program, perhaps with the capacity to call up a limited range of other applications programs, whilst staying in the one which has logged you on as user and is watching your connect-time and central processor usage.

One of the immediate aims of a serious hacker is to get out of this environment and see what other facilities might be located on the mainframe. For example, if access can be had to the user-log it becomes possible for the hacker to create a whole new status for himself, as a system manager, engineer, whatever. The new status, together with a unique new password, can have all sorts of privileges not granted to ordinary users. The hacker, having acquired the new status, logs out in his original identity and then logs back with his new one.

There is no single way to break out of an applications program into the operating system environment; people who do so seldom manage it by chance: they tend to have had some experience of a similar mainframe. One of the corny ways is to issue a BREAK or ctrl-C command and see what happens; but most applications programs concerned with logging users on to systems tend to filter out 'disturbing' commands of that sort. Sometimes it easier to go beyond the logging-in program into an another 'authorised' program and try to crash out of that. The usual evidence for success is that the nature of the prompts will change. Thus, on a well-known mini family OS, the usual user prompt is

COMMAND ?

or simply

>

Once you have crashed out the prompt may change to a simple

or

*

or even

:

it all depends.

To establish where you are in the system, you should ask for a
directory; DIR or its obvious variants often give results. Directories may be hierarchical, as in MS-DOS version 2 and above, so
that at the bottom level you simply get directories of other
directories. Unix machines are very likely to exhibit this trait. And
once you get a list of files and programs...well, that's where the
exploration really begins.

In 1982, two Los Angeles hackers, still in their teens, devised
one of the most sensational hacks so far, running all over the
Pentagon's ARPA data exchange network. ARPAnet was and is
the definitive packet-switched network (more about these in the
next chapter). It has been running for twenty years, cost more than
$500m and links together over 300 computers across the United
States and beyond. Reputedly it has 5,000 legitimate customers,
among them NORAD, North American Air Defence Headquarters at Omaha, Nebraska. Ron Austin and Kevin Poulsen were
determined to explore it.

Their weapons were an old TRS-80 and a VIC-20, nothing
complicated, and their first attempts relied on password-guessing.
The fourth try, 'UCB', the obvious initials of the University of
California at Berkeley, got them in. The password in fact was little
used by its legitimate owner and in the end, it was to be their
downfall.

Aspects of ARPAnet have been extensively written up in the
text-books simply because it has so many features which were first
tried there and have since become 'standard' on all data networks.
From the bookshop at UCLA, the hackers purchased the manual
for UNIX, the multi-tasking, multi-user operating system devised
by Bell Laboratories, the experimental arm of AT&T, the USA's
biggest telephone company. At the heart of Unix is a small kernel

containing system primitives; Unix instructions are enclosed in a series of shells, and very complicated procedures can be called in a small number of text lines simply by defining a few pipes linking shells. Unix also contains a large library of routines which are what you tend to find inside the shells. Directories of files are arranged in a tree-like fashion, with master or root directories leading to other directories, and so on.

Ron and Kevin needed to become system 'super-users' with extra privileges, if they were to explore the system properly; 'UCB' was merely an ordinary user. Armed with their knowledge of Unix, they set out to find the files containing legitimate users' passwords and names. Associated with each password was a Unix shell which defined the level of privilege. Ron wrote a routine which captured the privilege shell associated with a known super-user at the point when that user signed on and then dumped it into the shell associated with a little-used identity they had decided to adopt for their own explorations. They became 'Jim Miller'; the original super-user lost his network status. Other IDs were added. Captured privilege shells were hidden away in a small computer called Shasta at Stanford, at the heart of California's Silicon Valley.

Ron and Kevin were now super-users. They dropped into SRI, Stanford Research Institute, one of the world's great centres of scientific research; into the Rand Corporation, known equally for its extensive futurological forecasting and its 'thinking about the unthinkable', the processes of escalation to nuclear war; into the National Research Laboratory in Washington; into two private research firms back in California and two defence contractors on the East Coast; and across the Atlantic to the Norwegian Telecommunications Agency which, among other things, is widely believed to have a special role in watching Soviet Baltic activity. And, of course, NORAD.

Their running about had not gone unnoticed; ARPANet and its constituent computers keep logs of activity as one form of security (see the section below) and officials both at UCLA (where they were puzzled to see an upsurge in activity by 'UCB') and in one of the defence contractors sounded an alarm. The KGB were suspected, the FBI alerted.

One person asked to act as sleuth was Brian Reid, a professor of electrical engineering at Stanford. He and his associates set up a series of system trips inside a Unix shell to notify them when certain IDs entered an ARPANet computer. His first results seemed to indicate that the source of the hacking was Purdue, Indiana, but the strange IDs seemed to enter ARPANet from all over the place. Eventually, his researches lead him to the Shasta computer and he had identified 'Miller' as the identity he had to nail. He closed off entry to Shasta from ARPanet. 'Miller' reappeared; apparently via a gateway from another Stanford computer, Navajo. Reid, who in his sleuthing role had extremely high privileges, sought to wipe 'Miller' out of Navajo. A few minutes after 'Miller' had vanished from his screen, he reappeared from yet another local computer, Diablo. The concentration of hacking effort in the Stanford area lead Reid to suppose that the origin of the trouble was local. The most effective way to catch the miscreant was by telephone trace. Accordingly, he prepared some tantalising, apparently private, files. This was bait, designed to keep 'Miller' online as long as possible while the FBI organised a telephone trace. 'Miller' duly appeared, the FBI went into action — and arrested an innocent businessman.

But back at UCLA they were still puzzling about 'UCB'. In one of his earliest sessions, Ron had answered a registration questionnaire with his own address, and things began to fall into place. In one of his last computer 'chats' before arrest, Kevin, then only 17 and only beginning to think that he and his friend might have someone on their trail, is supposed to have signed off: 'Got to go now, the FBI is knocking at my door.' A few hours later, that is exactly what happened.

## Computer Security Methods

Hackers have to be aware of the hazards of being caught: there is now a new profession of computer security experts, and they have had some successes.

The first thing such consultants do is to attempt to divide responsibility within a computer establishment as much as possible. Only operators are allowed physical access to the installation, only programmers can use the operating system (and under some of these, such as VM, maybe only *part* of it.). Only system managers are permitted to validate passwords, and only the various classes of users are given access to the appropriate applications programs.

Next, if the operating system permits (it usually does), all accesses are logged; surveillance programs carry out an audit, which gives a historic record, and also, sometimes, perform monitoring, which is real-time surveillance.

In addition, separate programs may be in existence the sole purpose of which is threat monitoring: they test the system to see if anyone is trying repeatedly to log on without apparent success (say by using a program to try out various likely passwords). They assess if any one port or terminal is getting more than usual usage, or if IDs other than a regular small list start using a particular terminal — as when a hacker obtains a legitimate ID but one that normally operates from only one terminal within close proximity to the main installation, whereas the hacker is calling from outside.

Increasingly, in newer mainframe installations, security is built into the operating system at hardware level. In older models this was not done, partly because the need was not perceived, but also because each such 'unnecessary' hardware call tended to slow the whole machine down. (If a computer must encrypt and decrypt every process before it is executed, regular calculations and data accesses take much longer.) However, the largest manufacturers now seem to have found viable solutions for this problem....

# CHAPTER 7

# Networks

Until ten years ago, the telecommunications and computer industries were almost entirely separate. Shortly they will be almost completely fused. Most of today's hackers operate largely in ignorance of what goes on in the lines and switching centres between the computer they own and the computer they wish to access. Increasingly, dedicated hackers are having to acquire knowledge and experience of data networks, a task made more interesting, but not easier, by the fact that the world's leading telecommunications organisations are pushing through an unprecedented rate of innovation, both technical and commercial.

Apart from purely local lowspeed working, computer communications are now almost exclusively found on separate high-speed data networks, separate that is from the two traditional telecommunications systems telegraphy and telephone. Telex lines operate typically at 50 or 75 baud with an upper limit of 110 baud. The highest efficient speed for telephone-line-based data is 1200 baud. All of these are pitifully slow compared with the internal speed of even the most sluggish computer. When system designers first came to evaluate what sort of facilities and performance would be needed for data communications, it became obvious that relatively few lessons would be drawn from the solutions already worked out in voice communications.

### Analogue Networks

In voicegrade networks, the challenge had been to squeeze as many *analogue* signals down limited-size cables as possible. One of the earlier solutions, still very widely used, is frequency division multiplexing (FDM): each of the original speech paths is modulated onto one of a specific series of radio frequency carrier waves; each such rf wave is then suppressed at the transmitting source and reinserted close to the receiving position so that only one of the sidebands (the lower), the part that actually contains the intelligence of the transmission, is actually sent over the main data path. This is similar to ssb transmission in radio.

The entire series of suppressed carrier waves are then modulated onto a further carrier wave, which then becomes the main vehicle for taking the bundle of channels from one end of a line to the other. Typically, a small coaxial cable can handle 60 to 120 channels in this way, but large cables (the type dropped on the beds of oceans and employing several stages of modulation) can carry 2700 analogue channels. Changing audio channels (as they leave the telephone instrument and enter the local exchange) into rf channels, as well as making frequency division multiplexing possible, also brings benefits in that over long circuits it is easier to amplify rf signals to overcome losses in the cable.

Just before World War II, the first theoretical work was carried out to find further ways of economising on cable usage; what was then developed is called Pulse Code Modulation (PCM).

There are several stages. In the first, an analogue signal is sampled at specific intervals to produce a series of pulses; this is called Pulse Amplitude Modulation, and takes advantage of the characteristic of the human ear that if such pulses are sent down a line with only a very small interval between them, the brain smoothes over the gaps and reconstitutes the entire original signal. In the second stage, the levels of amplitude are sampled and translated into a binary code. The process of dividing an analogue signal into digital form and then reassembling it in analogue form is called quantization. Most PCM systems use 128 quantizing levels, each pulse being coded into 7 binary digits, with an eighth added for supervisory purposes.

**OPERATION OF A CHARACTER TDM**

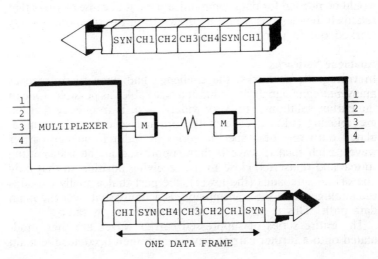

ONE DATA FRAME

70

By interleaving coded characters in a highspeed digital stream it is possible to send several separate voice channels along one physical link. This process is called Time Division Multiplexing (TDM) and together with FDM still forms the basis of most of the globe's voicegrade communications.

**Digital Networks**

Elegant though these solutions are, though, they are rapidly being replaced by totally digital schemes. Analogue systems would be very wasteful when all that is being transmitted are the discrete audio tones of the output of a modem. In a speech circuit, the technology has to be able to 'hear', receive, digitize and reassemble the entire audio spectrum between 100 Hz and 3000 Hz, which is the usual passband of what we have come to expect from the audio quality of the telephone. Moreover, the technology must be sensitive to a wide range of amplitude; speech is made up of pitch and associated loudness. In a digital network, however, all one really wants to transmit are the digits, and it doesn't matter whether they are signified by audio tones, radio frequency values, voltage conditions or light pulses, just so long as there is circuitry at either end which can encode and decode.

There are other problems with voice transmission: once two parties have made a connection with each other (by the one dialling a number and the other lifting a handset), good sense has suggested that it was desirable to keep a total physical path open between them, it not being practical to close down the path during silences and re-open it when someone speaks. In any case the electromechanical nature of most of today's phone exchanges would make such turning off and on very cumbersome and noisy. But with a purely digital transmission, routing of a 'call' doesn't have to be physical — individual blocks merely have to bear an electronic label of their originating and destination addresses, such addresses being 'read' in digital switching exchanges using chips, rather than electromechanical ones. Two benefits are thus simultaneously obtained: the valuable physical path (the cable or satellite link) is only in use when some intelligence is actually being transmitted, and is not in use during 'silence'; secondly, switching can be much faster and more reliable.

**Packet Switching**

These ideas were synthesised into creating what has now become packet switching. The methods were first described in the mid-1960s, but it was not until a decade later that suitable cheap technology existed to create a viable commercial service. The British Telecom product is called Packet SwitchStream (PSS) and notable comparable US services are Compuserve, Telenet and Tymnet. Many other countries have their own services and international packet switching is entirely possible — the UK service is called, unsurprisingly, IPSS.

## International Packet Switched Services and DNICs

### INTERNATIONAL NETWORKS

Datacalls can be made to hosts on any listed International Networks. The NIC (Data Network Identification Code) must precede the international host's NUA.
Charges quoted are for duration (per hour) and volume (per Ksegment) and are raised in steps of 1 minute and 10 segments respectively.

| Country | Network | DNIC |
|---|---|---|
| Australia | Midas | 5053 |
| Belgium | Euronet | 2062 |
| Belgium | Euronet | 2063 |
| Canada | Datapac | 3020 |
| Canada | Globedat | 3025 |
| Canada | Infoswitch | 3029 |
| Denmark | Euronet | 2383 |
| France | Transpac | 2080 |
| French Antilles | Euronet | 3400 |
| Germany (FDR) | Datex P | 2624 |
| Germany (FDR) | Euronet | 2623 |
| Hong Kong | IDAS | 4542 |
| Irish Republic | Euronet | 2723 |
| Italy | Euronet | 2223 |
| Japan | DDX-P | 4401 |
| Japan | Venus-P | 4408 |
| Luxembourg | Euronet | 2703 |
| Netherlands | Euronet | 2043 |

| Country | Network | DNIC |
|---|---|---|
| Norway | Norpak | 2422 |
| Portugal | N/A | 2682 |
| Singapore | Telepac | 5252 |
| South Africa | Saponet | 6550 |
| Spain | TIDA | 2141 |
| Sweden | Telepak | 2405 |
| Switzerland | Datalink | 2289 |
| Switzerland | Euronet | 2283 |
| U.S.A. | Autonet | 3126 |
| U.S.A. | Compuserve | 3132 |
| U.S.A. | ITT (UDTS) | 3103 |
| U.S.A. | RCA (LSDS) | 3113 |
| U.S.A. | Telenet | 3110 |
| U.S.A. | Tymnet | 3106 |
| U.S.A. | Uninet | 3125 |
| U.S.A. | WUI (DBS) | 3104 |

Additionally, Datacalls to the U.K. may be initiated from:

Bahrain, Barbados, Bermuda, Israel, New Zealand and the United Arabs Emirates.

Up to date information can be obtained from IPSS Marketing on 01-936 2743.

In essence, the service operates at 48kbits/sec full duplex (both directions simultaneously) and uses an extension of time division multiplexing. Transmission streams are separated in convenient-sized blocks or packets, each one of which contains a head and tail signifying origination and destination. The packets are assembled either by the originating computer or by a special facility supplied by the packet switch system. The packets in a single transmission stream may all follow the same physical path or may use alternate routes, depending on congestion. The packets from one 'conversation' are very likely to be interleaved with packets from many other 'conversations'. The originating and receiving computers see none of this. At the receiving end, the various packets are stripped of their routing information, and re-assembled in the correct order before presentation to the computer's VDU or applications program.

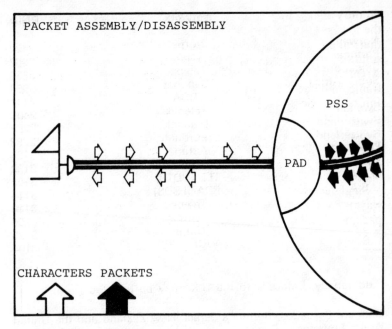

PACKET ASSEMBLY/DISASSEMBLY

PSS

PAD

CHARACTERS PACKETS

All public data networks using packet switching seek to be compatible with each other, at least to a considerable degree. The international standard they have to implement is called CCITT X.25. This is a multi-layered protocol covering (potentially) everything from electrical connections to the user interface.

The levels work like this:

7 APPLICATION   User interface

6 PRESENTATION Data formatting & code conversion

5 SESSION      Coordination between processes

4 TRANSPORT   Control of quality service

3 NETWORK     Set up and maintenance of connections

2 DATA LINK    Reliable transfer between terminal and network

1 PHYSICAL     Transfer of bitstream between terminal
              and network

At the moment international agreement has only been reached on the lowest three levels, Physical, Data Link and Network. Above that, there is a battle in progress between IBM, which has solutions to the problems under the name SNA (Systems Network Architecture) and most of the remainder of the principal mainframe manufacturers, whose solution is called OSI (Open Systems Interconnection).

## Packet Switching and the Single User

So much for the background explanation. How does this affect the user?

Single users can access packet switching in one of two principal ways. They can use special terminals able to create the data packets in an appropriate form — called Packet Terminals, in the

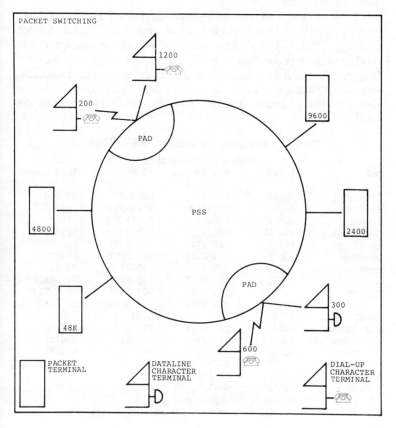

jargon — and these sit on the packet switch circuit, accessing it via the nearest PSS exchange using a permanent dataline and modems operating at speeds of 2400, 4800, 9600 or 48K baud, depending on level of traffic. Alternatively, the customer can use an ordinary asynchronous terminal without packet-creating capabilities, and connect into a special PSS facility which handles the packet assembly for him. Such devices are called Packet Assembler/ Disassemblers, or PADs. In the jargon, such users are said to have Character Terminals. PADs are accessed either via leased line at 300 or 1200, or via dial-up at those speeds, but also at 110 and 1200/75.

Most readers of this book, if they have used packet switching at all, will have done so using their own computers as character terminals and by dialling into a PAD. The phone numbers of UK PADs can be found in the PSS directory, published by Telecom National Networks.

In order to use PSS, you as an individual need a Network User Identity (NUI), which is registered at your local Packet Switch Exchange (PSE). The PAD at the PSE will throw you off if you don't give it a recognisable NUI. PADs are extremely flexible devices; they will configure their ports to suit your equipment, both as to speed and screen addressing, rather like a bulletin board (though to be accurate, it is the bulletin board which mimics the PAD).

## Phone numbers to access PSS PADs

| PSE | (STD) | Terminal operating speed: 110 OR 300 | 1200/75 | 1200 Duplex |
|---|---|---|---|---|
| Aberdeen | (0224) | 642242 | 642484 | 642644 |
| Birmingham | (021) | 2145139 | 2146191 | 241 3061 |
| Bristol | (0272) | 216411 | 216511 | 216611 |
| Cambridge | (0223) | 82511 | 82411 | 82111 |
| Edinburgh | (031) | 337 9141 | 337 9121 | 337 9393 |
| Glasgow | (041) | 204 2011 | 204 2031 | 204 2051 |
| Leeds | (0532) | 470711 | 470611 | 470811 |
| Liverpool | (051) | 211 0000 | 212 5127 | 213 6327 |
| London | (01) | 825 9421 | 407 8344 | 928 2333 |
| or | (01) | 928 9111 | 928 3399 | 928 1737 |
| Luton | (0582) | 8181 | 8191 | 8101 |
| Manchester | (061) | 833 0242 | 833 0091 | 833 0631 |
| Newcastle/Tyne | (0632) | 314171 | 314181 | 314161 |
| Nottingham | (0602) | 881311 | 881411 | 881511 |
| Portsmouth | (0705) | 53011 | 53911 | 53811 |
| Reading | (0734) | 389111 | 380111 | 384111 |
| *Slough | (0753) | 6141 | 6131 | 6171 |

*Local area code access to Slough is not available.
Switch the modem/dataphone to 'data' on receipt of data tone.

Next, you need the Network User Address (NUA) of the host you are calling. These are also available from the same directory: Cambridge University Computing Services's NUA is 234 222339399, BLAISE is 234 219200222, Istel is 234 252724241, and so on. The first four numbers are known as the DNIC (Data Network Identification Code); of these the first three are the country ('234' is the UK identifier), and the last one the specific service in that country, '2' signifying PSS. You can also get into Prestel via PSS, though for UK purposes it is an academic exercise: A9 234 1100 2018 gives you Prestel without the graphics (A9 indicates to the system that you have a teletype terminal). Once you have been routed to the host computer of your choice, then it is exactly if you were entering by direct dial; your password and so on will be requested.

Costs of using PSS are governed by the number of packets exchanged, rather than the distance between two computers or the actual time of the call. A typical PSS session will thus contain the following running costs: local phone call to PAD (on regular phone bill, time-related), PSS charges (dependent on number of packets sent) and host computer bills (which could be time-related or be per record accessed or on fixed subscription).

PACKET SWITCHED NETWORK

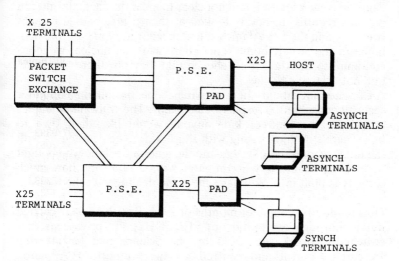

Packet switching techniques are not confined to public data networks: Prestel uses them for its own mini-network between the various Retrieval Computers (the ones the public dial into) and the Update and Mailbox Computers, and also to handle Gateway connections. Most newer private networks are packet switched.

Valued Added Networks (VANs) are basic telecoms networks or facilities to which some additional service — data processing or hosting of publishing ventures, for example — has been added.

Public Packet Switching, by offering easier and cheaper access, is a boon to the hacker. No longer does the hacker have to worry about the protocols that the host computer normally expects to see from its users. The X.25 protocol and the adaptability of the PAD mean that the hacker with even lowest quality asynchronous comms can talk to anything on the network. The tariff structure, favouring packets exchanged and not distance, means that any computer anywhere in the world can be a target.

Austin and Poulsen, the ARPAnet hackers, made dramatic use of a private packet-switched net; the Milwaukee 414s ran around GTE's Telenet service, one of the biggest public systems in the US. Their self-adopted name comes from the telephone area code for Milwaukee, a city chiefly known hitherto as a centre of the American beer industry. During the Spring and Summer of 1983, using publicly published directories, and the usual guessing games about pass-numbers and pass-words, the 414s dropped into the Security Pacific Bank in Los Angeles, the Sloan-Kettering Cancer Clinic in New York (it is still not clear to me if they actually altered patients records or merely looked at them), a Canadian cement company and the Los Alamos research laboratory in New Mexico, home of the atomic bomb, and where work on nuclear weapons continues to this day. It is believed that they saw there 'sensitive' but not 'classified' files.

Commenting about their activities, one prominent computer security consultant, Joesph Coates, said: 'The Milwaukee babies are great, the kind of kids anyone would like their own to be...There's nothing wrong with those kids. The problem is with the idiots who sold the system and the ignorant people who bought it. Nobody should buy a computer without knowing how much security is built in....You have the timid dealing with the foolish.'

During the first couple of months of 1984, British hackers carried out a thorough exploration of SERCNET, the private packet-switched network sponsored by the Science and Engineering Research Council and centred on the Rutherford Appleton Laboratory in Cambridge. It links together all the science and technology universities and polytechnics in the United Kingdom and has gateways to PSS and CERN (European Nuclear Research). Almost every type of mainframe and large mini-computer can be discovered hanging on to the system, IBM 3032 and 370 at Rutherford itself, Prime 400s, 550s and 750s all over the place, VAX 11/780s at Oxford, Daresbury, other VAXs at Durham, Cambridge, York, East Anglia and Newcastle, large numbers of GEC 4000 family members, and the odd PDP11 running Unix.

Penetration was first achieved when a telephone number appeared on a popular hobbyist bulletin board, together with the suggestion that the instruction 'CALL 40' might give results. It was soon discovered that if the hacker typed DEMO when asked for name and establishment, things started to happen. For several days hackers left each other messages on the hobbyist bulletin board, reporting progress, or the lack of it. Eventually, it became obvious that DEMO was supposed, as its name suggests, to be a limited facilities demonstration for casual users, but that it had been insecurely set up.

I can remember the night I pulled down the system manual, which had been left in an electronic file, watching page after page scroll down my VDU at 300 baud. All I had had to do was type the word 'GUIDE'. I remember also fetching down lists of addresses and mnemonics of SERCNET members. Included in the manual were extensive descriptions of the network protocols and their relation to 'standard' PSS-style networks.

As I complete this chapter I know that certain forms of access to SERCNET have been shut off, but that hacker exploration appears to continue. Some of the best hacker stories do not have a definite ending. I offer some brief extracts from captured SERCNET sessions.

```
83E028aae NODE 3.
Which Service?
PAD
COM
PAD>CALL 40
Welcome to SERCNET-PSS Gateway. Type HELP for help.

Gatewx~c!nkging in
user HELP
ID last used Wednesday, 18 January 1984 16:53
Started - Wed 18 Jan 1984 17:07:58
Please enter your name and establishment DEMO
Due to a local FTP problem, messages entered via the HELP system
during the last month have been lost. Please resubmit if problem/question
is still outstanding  9/1/84

No authorisation is required for calls which do not incur charges at the
Gateway.  There is now special support for TELEX.  A TELEX service
may be announced shortly.

Copies of the PSS Guide issue 4 are available on request to Program
Advisory Office at RAL, telephone 0235 44 6111 (direct dial in) or
0235 21900 Ext 6111.  Requests for copies should no longer be placed
in this help system.

The following options are available:
```

```
NOTES  GUIDE  TITLES  ERRORS  EXAMPLES  HELP  QUIT
Which option do you require? GUIDE
The program 'VIEW' is used to display the Gateway guide
Commands available are:
<CR> or N        next page
P                previous page
n                list page n
+n or -n         go forward or back n pages
S                first page
E                last page
L/string         find line containing string
F/string         find line beginning string
Q                exit from VIEW




VIEW Vn 6> Q
The following options are available:

NOTES  GUIDE  TITLES  ERRORS  EXAMPLES  HELP  QUIT
Which option do you require? HELP
NOTES    replies to user quries & other notes
GUIDE    is the complete Gateway user guide (including the Appendices)
TITLES   is a list of SERCNET & PSS addresses & mnemonics (Guide Appendix 1)
ERRORS   List of error codes you may receive
EXAMPLES are some examples of use of the Gateway (Guide Appendix 2)
HELP     is this
QUIT     exits from this session
The following options are available:

NOTES  GUIDE  TITLES  ERRORS  EXAMPLES  HELP  QUIT
Which option do you require? TITLES




VIEW Vn 6>

If you have any comments, please type them now, terminate with E
on a line on its own. Otherwise just type <cr>

CPU used: 2 ieu, Elapsed: 14 mins, IO: 2380 units, Breaks: 114
Budgets: this period = 32.000 AUs, used = 0.015 AUs, left = 29.161 AUs
User HELP   terminal   2 logged out  Wed 18 Jan 1984 17:21:59


  84/01/18. 18.47.00.
  I.C.C.C. NETWORK OPERATING SYSTEM.      NOS 1.1-430.20A
USER NUMBER:
PASSWORD
████████
IMPROPER LOG IN, TRY AGAIN.
USER NUMBER:
PASSWORD
>
>
>SCIENCE AND ENGINEERING RESEARCH COUNCIL
>
>RUTHERFORD APPLETON LABORATORY
>COMPUTING DIVISION
>
>
>
>                      The SERCNET - PSS Gateway
>
>                           User's Guide
>
>
>                                                        A S Dunn
>                                                  16 February 1983
>Issue 4
>
>
>
>
>Introduction
>
```

>The SERCNET-PSS Gateway provides access from  SERCNET  to  PSS  and  PSS  to
>SERCNET.   It  functions  as  a  'straight  through'  connection between the
>networks, ie it is protocol transparant.  It operates as a  Transport  Level
>gateway,  in  accordance  with  the  'Yellow Book' Transport Service. However
>the present implementation does not have  a  full  Transport  Service,  and
>therefore there are some limitations in the service provided.  For X29 which
>is incompatible with the Yellow Book Transport Service,  special  facilities
>are provided for the input of user identification and addresses.
>
>No protocol conversion facilities are provided by  the  Gateway  -  protocol
>conversion  facilities  (eg X29 - TS29) can be provided by calling through a
>third party machine (usually on SERCNET).
>
>The Transport Service addressing has been extended to include  authorisation
>fields, so that users can be billed for any charges they incur.
>
>The Gateway also provides facilities for users to inspect their accounts and
>change their passwords, and also a limited HELP facility.
>
>User Interface
>
>The interface which the user sees will depend  on  the  local  equipment  to
>which he  is attached.  This may be a PAD in which case he will probably be
>using the X29 protocol, or a HOST (DTE) in which case he might be using  FTP
>for  example.   The  local  equipment  must  have  some way of generating a
>Transport Service Called Address for the Gateway,  which  also  includes  an
>authorisation  field  -  the  format  of  this  is described below.   The
>documentation for the local system must therefore be consulted in  order  to
>find  out  how  to  generate  the  Transport  Service Called Address.  Some
>examples are given in Appendix 2.
>
>A facility is provided for the benefit of users without access to the  'Fast
>Select'  facility,  eg BT PAD users, (but available to all X29 terminal users)
>whereby either a minimal address can be included in the Call User Data Field
>or  an  X25 subaddress can be used and the Call User Data Field left absent.
>
>                             - 1 -
>
>The authorisation and address can then  be  entered  when  prompted  by  the
>Gateway.
>
>
>Unauthorised Use
>.
>No unauthorised use of the Gateway is allowed regardless of whether  charges
>are incurred at the Gateway or not.
>
>However, there is an account DEMO (password will  be  supplied  on  request)
>with a small allocation which is available for users to try out the Gateway,
>but it should be noted that excessive use of this account will soon  exhaust
>the allocation, thus depriving others of its use.
>
>Prospective users of the Gateway should first contact User  Interface  Group
>in the Computing Division of the Rutherford Appleton Laboratory.
>
>
>Addressing
>
>To connect a call through the Gateway, the following information is required
>in the Transport Service Called Address:
>
>1)    The name of the called network
>2)    Authorisation, consisting of  a  USERID,  PASSWORD  and  ACCOUNT,  and
>      optionally, a reverse charging request
>3)    The address of the target host on the called network
>
>The format is as follows:
>
><netname>(<authorisation>).<host address>
>
>
>1)    <Netname> is one of the following:

81

```
>SERCNET              to connect to the SERC network
>PSS                  to connect to PSS
>S                    an alias for SERCNET
>69                   another alias for SERCNET
>
>
>2)       <Authorisation> is a list of positional or keyword parameters  or
>booleans as follows:
>
>Keyword              Meaning
>
>US                   User identifier
>PW                   User's password
>AC                   the account - not used at present - taken to be same as US
Frm   5; Next>
>RP                   'reply paid' request (see below)
>R                    reverse charging indicator (boolean)
>
>Keywords are separated from their values by '='.
>Keyword-value pairs, positional parameters and booleans are  separated  from
>each other by ','. The whole string is enclosed in parentheses: ().
>
>
>                              - 2 -
>Examples:
>
>(FRED,XYZ,R)
>(US=FRED,PW=XYZ,R)
>(R,PW=XYZ,US=FRED)
>
>All the above have exactly the same meaning.  The first  form  is  the  most
>usual.
>
>When using positionals, the order is: US,PW,AC,RP,R
>
Frm   6; Next>
>
>3)       <Host address> is the address of the machine being called  on  the
>target network.  It may be a compound address, giving the service within the
>target machine to be used.  It may begin with a mnemonic instead of  a  full
>DTE address.  A list of current mnemonics for both SERCNET and PSS is given
>in Appendix 1.
>
>A restriction of using the Gateway is that where a Transport Service address
>(service  name) is required by the target machine to identify the service to
>be used, then this must be included explicitly by the user in the  Transport
>Service Called Address, and not assumed from the mnemonic, since the Gateway
>cannot know from the mnemonic, which protocol is being used.
>
>Examples:
>
>RLGB.FTP
>4.FTP
>
>Both the above would refer to the FTP service on  the  GEC  'B'  machine  at
>Rutherford.
>
>RLGB alone would in fact connect to the X29 server, since no service name is
Frm   7; Next>
>required for X29.
>
>
>In order  to  enable  subaddresses  to  be  entered  more  easily  with  PSS
>addresses,  the  delimiter  '-'  can be used to delimit a mnemonic. When the
>mnemonic is translated to an address the delimiting '-' is deleted  so  that
>the following string is combined with the address. Eg:
>
>SERC-99 is translated to 23422351919199
>
>
>
>Putting the abovementioned  three  components  together,  a  full  Transport
>Service Called Address might look like:
>
>S(FRED,XYZ,R).RLGB.FTP
```

82

>Of course a request for reverse charging on SERCNET is meaningless, but not
>illegal.
>
>Reply Paid Facility        (Omit at first reading)
>
>In many circumstances it is necessary for temporary authorisation to be
>passed to a third party. For example, the recipient of network MAIL may not
>himself be authorised to use the Gateway, and therefore the sender may wish
>to grant him temporary authorisation in order to reply. With the Job
>Transfer and Maniplulation protocol, there is a requirement to return
>output documents from jobs which have been executed on a remote site.
>
>The reply paid facility is invoked by including the RP keyword in the
>authorisation. It can be used either as a boolean or as a keyword-value
>pair. When used as a boolean, a default value of 1 is assumed.
>
>The value of the RP parameter indicates the number of reply paid calls which
>are to be authorised. All calls which use the reply paid authorisation will
>be charged to the account of the user who initiated the reply paid
>authorisation.
Frm    9; Next>
>
>The reply paid authorisation parameters are transmitted to the destination
>address of a call as a temporary user name and password in the Transport
>Service Calling Address. The temporary user name and password are in a form
>available for use by automatic systems in setting up a reply to the address
>which initiated the original call.
>
>Each time a successful call is completed using the temporary user name and
>password, the number of reply paid authorisations is reduced by 1, until
>there are none left, when no further replies are allowed. In addition there
>is an expiry date of 1 week, after which the authorisations are cancelled.
>
>In the event of call failures and error situations, it is important that the
>effects are clearly defined. In the following definitions, the term 'fail'
>is used to refer to any call which terminates with either a non-zero
>clearing cause or diagnostic code or both, regardless of whether data has
>been communicated or not. The rules are defined as follows:
>
>1)    If a call which has requested reply paid authorisation fails for any
>      reason, then the reply paid authorisation is not set up.
>
>2)    If the Gateway is unable to set up the reply paid authorisation for
Frm    10; Next>
>      any reason (eg insufficient space), then the call requesting the
>      authorisation will be refused.
>
>3)    A call which is using reply paid authorisation may not create another
>      reply paid authorisation.
>
>4)    If a call which is using reply paid authorisation fails due to a
>      network error (clearing cause non zero) then the reply paid count is
>      not reduced.
>
>5)    If a call which is using reply paid authprisation fails due to a host
>      clearing (clearing cause zero, diagnostic code non-zero) then the
>      reply paid count is reduced, except where the total number of segments
>      transferred on the call is zero (ie call setup was never completed).
>
Frm    11; Next>
>
>X29 Terminal Protocol
>
>There is a problem in that X29 is incompatible with the Transport Service.
>For this reason, it is possible that some PAD implementations will be unable
>to generate the Transport Service Called Address. Also some PAD's, eg the
>British Telecom PAD, may be unable to generate Fast Select calls - this
>means that the Call User Data Field is only 12 bytes long - insufficient to
>hold the Transport Service Address.
>
>If a PAD is able to insert a text string into the Call User Data Field,
>beginning at the fifth byte, but is restricted to 12 characters because of
>inability to generate Fast Select calls, then a partial address can be
>included, consisting of either the network name being called, or the network
>name plus authorisation.

```
>
>The first character is treated as a delimiter, and should be entered as  the
>character 'ə'. This is followed by the name of the called network - SERCNET,
>S or PSS.
>
>Alternatively, if the PAD is incapable of generating a Call User Data Field,
>then  the  network  name can be entered as an X25 subaddress.  The mechanism
Frm   12; Next>
>employed by the Gateway is to transcribe the X25 subaddress to the beginning
>of  the  Transport  Service  Called  Address,  converting  the digits of the
>subaddress into ASCII characters in the process.  Note that this means  only
>SERCNET can be called with this method at present by using subaddress 69.
>
>
>The response from the Gateway will be the following message:
>
>Please enter your authorisation and address required in form:
>(user,password).address
>>
>
>Reply with the appropriate response eg:
>
>(FRED,XYZ).RLGB
>
>There is a timeout of between 3 and 4 minutes for this response, after which
>the call will be cleared.  There is no limit to the number of attempts which
>may be made within this time limit - if the authorisation or address entered
>is  invalid, the Gateway will request it again.  To abandon the attempt, the
>call should be cleared from the local PAD.
>
Frm   13; Next>
>A restriction of this method of use of the Gateway is that a  call  must  be
>correctly  authorised by the Gateway before charging can begin, thus reverse
>charge calls from PSS which do not contain authorisation in the Call Request
>packet.  However it is possible to include the authorisation
>but not the address in the Call Request packet.  The authorisation must then
>be entered again together with the address when requested by the Gateway.
>
>The above also applies when using a  subaddress  to  identify  the  called
>network.  In  this  case  the  Call  User  Data Field will contain only the
>authorisation in parentheses (preceded by the delimiter 'ə')
>
>
>_                                  - 5 -
```

```
.
>
>Due to the lack of a Transport Service ACCEPT primitive in X29, it  will  be
>found,  on  some  PADs, that  a 'call connected' message will appear on the
>terminal as soon as the call has been connected to the  Gateway.  The  'call
>connected'  message  should not be taken to imply that contact has been made
>with the ultimate destination.  The Gateway  will  output  a  message  'Call
>connected to remote address' when the connection has been established.
>
Frm   14; Next>
>
>ITP Terminal Protocol
>
>The terminal protocol ITP is used extensively on  SERCNET,  and  some  hosts
>support  only  this terminal protocol.  Thus it will not be possible to make
>calls directly between these hosts on SERCNET and addresses  on  PSS  which
>support only X29 or TS29.  In these cases it will be necessary to go through
⇒an intermediate machine on SERCNET which supports both X29 and ITP  or  TS29
>and  ITP,  such  as a GEC MUM.  This is done by first making a call to the GEC
>MUM, and then making an outgoing call from there to the desired destination.
>
>
>TS29 Terminal Protocol
>
>This is the ideal protocol to use through the Gateway, since there should be
>no  problem  about  entering  the  Transport Service address.  However, it is
>advisable first to ascertain that the machine to  be  called  will  support
>TS29.
>
>When using this protocol, the service name of  the  TS29  server  should  be
>entered explicitly, eg:
```

84

```
Frm    15; Next>
>S(FRED,XYZ).RLGB.TS29
>
>
>Restrictions
>
>Due to the present lack of a full Transport Service  in  the  Gateway,  some
>primitives are not fully supported.
>
>In particular, the ADDRESS, DISCONNECT and RESET primitives  are  not  fully
>supported.   However  this  should  not  present serious problems, since the
>ADDRESS and RESET  primitives  are  not  widely  used,  and  the  DISCONNECT
>primitive can be carried in a Clear Request packet.
>
>
>IPSS
>
>Access to IPSS is through PSS.  Just enter the IPSS address in place of  the
>PSS address.
>
>
```

        ................and on and on for 17 pages........

# CHAPTER 8

# Viewdata Systems

Viewdata, or videotex, has had a curious history. At one stage, in the late 1970s, it was possible to believe that it was about to take over the world, giving computer power to the masses via their domestic tv sets. It was revolutionary in the time it was developed, around 1975, in research laboratories owned by what was then called the Post Office, but which is now British Telecom. It had a colour-and-graphics display, a user-friendly means of talking to it at a time when most computers needed precise grunts to make them work, and the ordinary layperson could learn how to use it in five minutes.

The viewdata revolution never happened, because Prestel, its most public incarnation, was mismarketed by its owners, British Telecom, and because, in its original version, it is simply too clumsy and limited to handle more sophisticated applications. All information is held on electronic file cards which can easily be either too big or too small for a particular answer and the only way you can obtain the desired information is by keying numbers, trundling down endless indices. In the early days of Prestel, most of what you got was indices, not substantive information. By the time that viewdata sets were supposed to exist in their hundreds of thousands, home computers, which had not been predicted at all when viewdata first appeared, had already sold into the millionth British home.

Yet private viewdata, mini-computers configured to look like Prestel and to use the same special terminals, has been a modest success. At the time of writing there are between 120 and 150 significant installations. They have been set up partly to serve the needs of individual companies, but also to help particular trades, industries and professions. The falling cost of viewdata terminals has made private systems attractive to the travel trade, to retail stores, the motor trade, to some local authorities and to the financial world.

The hacker, armed with a dumb viewdata set, or with a software 'fix' for his micro, can go ahead and explore these services. At the beginning of this book, I said my first hack was of a viewdata service, Viditel, the Dutch system. It is astonishing how many British hackers have had a similar experience. Indeed, the habit of viewdata hacking has spread throughout Europe also: the wonderfully named Chaos Computer Club of Hamburg had some well-publicised fun with Bildschirmtext, the West German Prestel equivalent colloquially-named Btx.

What they appear to have done was to acquire the password of the Hamburger Sparkasse, the country's biggest savings bank group. Whereas telebanking is a relatively modest part of Prestel — the service is called Homelink — the West German banks have been a powerful presence on Btx since its earliest days. In fact, another Hamburg bank, the Verbraucher Bank, was responsible for the world's first viewdata Gateway, for once in this technology, showing the British the way. The 25-member Computer Chaos Club probably acquired the password as a result of the carelessness of a bank employee. Having done so, they set about accessing the bank's own, rather high priced, pages, some of which cost almost DM10 (£2.70). In a deliberate demonstration, the Club then set a computer to systematically call the pages over and over again, achieving a re-access rate of one page every 20 seconds. During a weekend in mid-November 1984, they made more than 13,000 accesses and ran up a notional bill of DM135,000 (£36,000). Information Providers, of course, are not charged for looking at their own pages, so no bill was payable and the real cost of the hack was embarrassment.

In hacking terms, the Hamburg hack was relatively trivial — simple password acquisition. Much more sophisticated hacks have been perpertrated by British enthusiasts.

Viewdata hacking has three aspects: to break into systems and become user, editor or system manager thereof; to discover hidden parts of systems to which you have been legitimately admitted, and to uncover new services.

## Viewdata software structures

An understanding of how a viewdata database is set up is a great aid in learning to discover what might be hidden away.

Remember, there are always two ways to each page — by following the internal indexes, or by direct keying using *nnn#. In typical viewdata software, each electronic file card or 'page' exists on an overall tree-like structure:

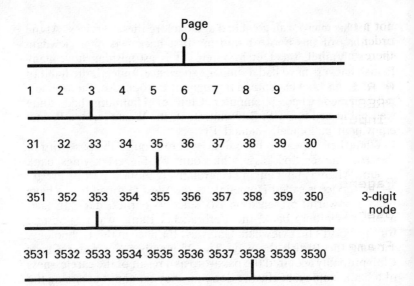

Page
0

1    2    3    4    5    6    7    8    9

31  32  33  34  35  36  37  38  39  30

351  352  353  354  355  356  357  358  359  350    3-digit node

3531 3532 3533 3534 3535 3536 3537 3538 3539 3530

Top pages are called parents; lower pages filials. Thus page 3538 needs parent pages 353, 35, 3 and 0 to support it, i.e. these pages must exist on the system. On Prestel, the parents owned by Information Providers (the electronic publishers) are 3 digits long (3-digit nodes). Single and double-digit pages (0 to 99) are owned by the 'system manager' (and so are any pages beginning with the sequences 100nn–199nn and any beginning with a 9nnn). When a page is set up by an Information Provider (the process of going into 'edit' mode varies from software package to package; on Prestel, you call up page 910) two processes are necessary — the overt page (i.e. the display the user sees) must be written using a screen editor. Then the IP must select a series of options — e.g. whether the page is for gathering a response from the user or is just to furnish information; whether the page is to be open for viewing by all, by a Closed User Group, or just by the IP (this facility is used while a large database is being written and so that users don't access part of it by mistake); the price (if any) the page will bear — and the 'routing instructions'. When you look at a viewdata page and it says 'Key 8 for more information on ABC', it is the routing table that is constructed during edit that tells the viewdata computer: 'If a user on this page keys 8, take him through to the following next page'. Thus, page 353880 may say 'More information on ABC....KEY 8'. The information on ABC is actually held on page 3537891. The routing table on page 353880 will say: 8=3537891. In this example, you will see that 3537891 is not a true filial of 353880 — this does not matter; however, in order for 3537891 to exist on the system, *its* parents must exist, i.e. there must be pages 353789, 35378, 3537 etc.

```
P R E S T E L
PRESTEL EDITING SYSTEM
 Input Details -

              Update option    o

Pageno    4190100          Frame-Id    a

User CUG                   User access    y

Frame type   i             Frame price        2p

           Choice type    s

Choices
  0-   *              1-    4196121
  2-   4196118        3-    4196120
  4-   4196112        5-    4196119
  6-   4196110        7-    *
  8-   4190101        9-    4199
```

**Prestel Editing. This is the 'choices' page which sets up the frame before the overt page – the one the user sees – is prepared.**

These quirky features of viewdata software can help the hacker search out hidden databases:

● Using a published directory, you can draw up a list of 'nodes' and who occupies them. You can then list out apparently 'unoccupied' nodes and see if they contain anything interesting. It was when a hacker spotted that an 'obvious' Prestel node, 456, had been unused for a while, that news first got out early in 1984 about the Prestel Microcomputing service, several weeks ahead of the official announcement.

● If you look at the front page of a service, you can follow the routeings of the main index — are all the obvious immediate filials used? If not, can you get at them by direct keying?

- Do any services start lower down a tree than you might expect (i.e. more digits in a page number than you might have thought)? In that case, try accessing the parents and see what happens.

- Remember that you can get a message 'no such page' for two reasons: because the page really doesn't exist, or because the Information Provider has put it on 'no user access'. In the latter case, check to see whether this has been done consistently — look at the immediate possible filials. To go back to when Prestel launched its Prestel Microcomputing service, using page 456 as a main node, 456 itself was closed off until the formal opening, but page 45600 was open.

## Prestel Special Features

In general, this book has avoided giving specific hints about individual services, but Prestel is so widely available in the UK and so extensive in its coverage that a few generalised notes seem worthwhile.

Not all Prestel's databases may be found via the main index or in the printed directories; even some that are on open access are unadvertised. Of particular interest over the last few years have been nodes 640 (owned by the Research and Development team at Martlesham), 651 (Scratchpad — used for ad hoc demonstration databases), 601 (mostly mailbox facilities but also known to carry experimental advanced features so that they can be tried out), and 650 (News for Information Providers — mostly but not exclusively in a Closed User Group). Occasionally equipment manufacturers offer experimental services as well: I have found high-res graphics and even instruction codes for digitised full video lurking around.

In theory, what you find on one Prestel computer you will find on all the others. In practice this has never been true, as it has always been possible to edit individually on each computer, as well as on the main updating machine which is supposed to broadcast to all the others. The differences in what is held in each machine will become greater over time.

Gateway is a means of linking non-viewdata external computers to the Prestel system. It enables on-screen buying and booking, complete with validation and confirmation. It even permits telebanking. Most 'live' forms of gateway are very secure, with several layers of password and security. However, gateways require testing before they can be offered to the public; in the past,

hackers have been able to secure free rides out of Prestel....
Careful second-guessing of the routings on the databases including telesoftware* have given users free programs while the telesoftware* was still being tested and before actual public release.

Prestel, as far as the ordinary user is concerned, is a very secure system — it uses 14-digit passwords and disconnects after three unsuccessful tries. For most purposes, the only way of hacking into Prestel is to acquire a legitimate user's password, perhaps because they have copied it down and left it prominently displayed. Most commercial viewdata sets allow the owner to store the first ten digits in the set (some even permit the full 14), thus making the casual hacker's task easier.

However, Prestel was sensationally hacked at the end of October 1984, the whole system lying at the feet of a team of four West London hackers for just long enough to demonstrate the extent of their skill to the press. Their success was the result of persistence and good luck on their side and poor security and bad luck on the part of BT. As always happens with hacking activities that do not end up in court, some of the details are disputed; there are also grounds for believing that news of the hack was deliberately held back until remedial action had taken place, but this is the version I believe:

The public Prestel service consists of a network of computers, mostly for access by ordinary users, but with two special-purpose machines, Duke for IPs to update their information into and Pandora, to handle Mailboxes (Prestel's variant on electronic mail). The computers are linked by non-public packet-switched lines. Ordinary Prestel users are registered (usually) onto two or three computers local to them which they can access with the simple three-digit telephone number 618 or 918. In most parts of the UK, these two numbers will return a Prestel whistle. (BT Prestel have installed a large number of local telephone nodes and

---

*Telesoftware is a technique for making regular computer programs available via viewdata: the program lines are compressed according to a simple set of rules and set up on a series of viewdata frames. Each frame contains a modest error-checking code. To receive a program, the user's computer, under the control of a 'download' routine, calls the first program page down from the viewdata host, runs the error check on it, and demands a retransmission if the check gives a 'false'. If it gives a 'true', the user's machine unsqueezes the program lines and dumps them into the computer's main memory or disc store. It then requests the next viewdata page until the whole program is collected. You then have a text file which must be converted into program instructions. Depending on what model of micro you have, and which telesoftware package, you can either run the program immediately or 'exec' it. Personally I found the telesoftware experience interesting the first time I tried it, and quite useless in terms of speed, reliability and quality afterwards.

leased lines to transport users to their nearest machine at local call rates, even though in some cases that machine may be 200 miles away). Every Prestel machine also has several regular phone numbers associated with it, for IPs and engineers. Most of these numbers confer no extra privileges on callers: if you are registered to a particular computer and get in via a 'back-door' phone number you will pay Prestel and IPs exactly the same as if you had dialled 618 or 918. If you are not registered, you will be thrown off after three tries.

In addition to the public Prestel computers there are a number of other BT machines, not on the network, which look like Prestel and indeed carry versions of the Prestel database. These machines, left over from an earlier stage of Prestel's development, are now used for testing and development of new Prestel features. The old Hogarth computer, originally used for international access, is now called 'Gateway Test' and, as its name implies, is used by IPs to try out the interconnections of their computers with those of Prestel prior to public release. It is not clear how the hackers first became aware of the existence of these 'extra' machines; one version is that it was through the acquisition of a private phone book belonging to a BT engineer. Another version suggests that they tried 'obvious' log-in pass-numbers — 2222222222 1234 — on a public Prestel computer and found themselves inside a BT internal Closed User Group which contained lists of phone numbers for the develop computers. The existence of at least two stories suggests that the hackers wished to protect their actual sources. In fact, some of the phone numbers had, to my certain knowledge, appeared previously on bulletin boards.

At this first stage, the hackers had no passwords; they could simply call up the log-in page. Not being registered on that computer, they were given the usual three tries before the line was disconnected.

For a while, the existence of these log-in pages was a matter of mild curiosity. Then, one day, in the last week of October, one of the log-in pages looked different: it contained what appeared to be a valid password, and one with system manager status, no less. A satisfactory explanation for the appearance of this password imprinted on a log-in page has not so far been forthcoming. Perhaps it was carelessness on the part of a BT engineer who thought that, as the phone number was unlisted, no unauthorised individual would ever see it. The pass-number was tried and admission secured. After a short period of exploration of the database, which appeared to be a 'snapshot' of Prestel rather than a live version of it — thus showing that particular computer was not receiving constant updates from Duke — the hackers decided to explore the benefits of System Manager status. Since they had between them some freelance experience of editing on Prestel, they knew that all Prestel special features pages are in the *9nn# range: 910 for editing; 920 to change personal passwords; 930 for mailbox messages and so ...what would pages 940, 950, 960 and so on do? It became obvious that these pages would reveal details of users together with account numbers (systelnos), passwords and personal passwords. There were facilities to register and deregister users.

However, all this was taking place on a non-public computer. Would the same passwords on a 'live' Prestel machine give the same benefits? Amazingly enough, the passwords gave access to every computer on the Prestel network. It was now time to examine the user registration details of real users as opposed to the BT employees who were on the development machine. The hackers were able to assume any personality they wished and could thus enter any Closed User Group, simply by picking the right name. Among the CUG services they swooped into were high-priced ones providing investment advice for clients of the stockbroker Hoare Govett and commentary on international currency markets supplied by correspondents of the *Financial Times*. They were also able to penetrate Homelink, the telebanking service run by the Nottingham Building Society. They were not able to divert sums of money, however, as Homelink uses a series of security checks which are independent of the Prestel system.

Another benefit of being able to become whom they wished was the ability to read Prestel Mailboxes, both messages in transit that had not yet been picked up by the intended recipient and those that had been stored on the system once they had been read. Among the Mailboxes read was the one belonging to Prince Philip. Later, with a newspaper reporter as witness, one hacker sent a Mailbox, allegedly from Prince Philip to the Prestel System Manager:

I do so enjoy puzzles and games. Ta ta. Pip! Pip!

H R H Hacker

Newspaper reports also claimed that the hackers were able to gain editing passwords belonging to IPs, enabling them to alter pages and indeed the *Daily Mail* of November 2nd carried a photograph of a Prestel page from the *Financial Times International Financial Alert* saying:

The FT maintained that, whatever might theoretically have been possible, in fact they had no record of their pages actually being so altered and hazarded the suggestion that the hacker, having broken into their CUG and accessed the page, had 'fetched it back' onto his own micro and then edited there, long enough for the *Mail's* photographer to snap it for his paper, but without actually retransmitting the false page back to Prestel. As with so many other hacking incidents, the full truth will never be known because no one involved has any interest in its being told.

However, it is beyond doubt that the incident was regarded wth the utmost seriousness by Prestel itself. They were convinced of the extent of the breach when asked to view page 1, the main index page, which bore the deliberate mis-spelling: Idnex. Such a change theoretically could only have been made by a Prestel employee with the highest internal security clearance. Within 30 minutes, the system manager password had been changed on all computers, public and research. All 50,000 Prestel users signing on immediately after November 2nd were told to change their personal password without delay on every computer to which they were registered. And every IP received, by Special Delivery, a complete set of new user and editing passwords.

Three weeks after the story broke, the *Daily Mail* thought it had found yet another Prestel hack and ran the following page 1 headline: 'Royal codebuster spies in new raid on Prestel', a wondrous collection of headline writer's buzzwords to capture the attention of the sleepy reader. This time an Information Provider was claiming that, even after new passwords had been distributed, further security breaches had occurred and that there was a 'mole' within Prestel itself. That evening, Independent Television News ran a feature much enjoyed by cognoscenti: although the story was about the Prestel service, half the film footage used to illustrate it was wrong: they showed pictures of the Oracle (teletext) editing facility and of some-one using a keypad that could only have belonged to a TOPIC set, as used for the Stock Exchange's private service. Finally, the name of the expert pulled in for interview was mis-spelled although he was a well-known author of micro books. The following day, BBC-tv's breakfast show ran an item on the impossibility of keeping Prestel secure, also full of ludicrous inaccuracies.

It was the beginning of a period during which hackers and hacking attracted considerable press interest. No news service operating in the last two months of 1984 felt it was doing an effective job if it couldn't feature its own Hacker's Confession, suitably filmed in deep shadow. As happens now and again, press enthusiasm for a story ran ahead of the ability to check for accuracy and a number of Hacks That Never Were were reported and, in due course, solemnly commented on.

BT had taken much punishment for the real hack — as well as causing deep depression among Prestel staff, the whole incident had occurred at the very point when the corporation was being privatised and shares being offered for sale to the public — and to suffer an unwarranted accusation of further lapses in security was just more than they could bear.

It is unlikely that penetration of Prestel to that extent will ever happen again, though where hacking is concerned, *nothing* is impossible.

There is one, relatively uncommented-upon vulnerability in the present Prestel set-up: the information on Prestel is most easily altered via the bulk update protocols used by Information Providers, where there is a remarkable lack of security. All the system presently requires is a 4-character editing password and the IP's systel number, which is usually the same as his mailbox number (obtainable from the on-system mailbox directory on page *7#) which in turn is very likely to be derived from a phone number.

## Other viewdata services

Large numbers of other viewdata services exist: in addition to the Stock Exchange's TOPIC and the other viewdata based services mentioned in chapter 4, the travel trade has really clutched the technology to its bosom: the typical High Street agent not only accesses Prestel but several other services which give up-to-date information on the take-up of holidays, announce price changes and allow confirmed air-line and holiday bookings.

Several of the UK's biggest car manufacturers have a stock locator system for their dealers: if you want a British Leyland model with a specific range of accessories and in the colour combinations of your choice, the chances are that your local dealer will not have it stock. He can, however, use the stock locator to tell him with which other dealer such a machine may be found.

Stock control and management information is used by retail chains using, in the main, a package developed by a subsidiary of Debenhams. Debenhams had been early enthusiasts of Prestel in the days when it was still being pitched at a mass consumer audience — its service was called Debtel which wags suggested was for people who owed money or, alternatively, for upper-class young ladies. Later it formed DISC to link together its retail outlets, and this was hacked in 1983. The store denied that anything much had happened, but the hacker appeared (in shadow) on a tv program together with a quite convincing demonstration of his control over the system.

Audience research data is despatched in viewdata mode to advertising agencies and broadcasting stations by AGB market research.

There are even alternate viewdata networks rivalling that owned by Prestel, the most important of which is, at the time of writing, the one owned by Istel and headquartered at Redditch in the Midlands. This network transports several different trade and professional services as well as the internal data of British Leyland, of whom Istel is a subsidiary.

A viewdata *front-end processor* is a minicomputer package which sits between a conventionally-structured database and its ports which look into the phone-lines. Its purpose is to allow users with viewdata sets to search the main database without the need to purchase an additional conventional dumb terminal. Some viewdata front-end processors (FEPs) expect the user to have a full alphabetic keyboard, and merely transform the data into viewdata pages 40 characters by 24 lines in the usual colours. More sophisticated FEPs go further and allow users with only numeric keypads to retrieve information as well. By using FEPs a database publisher or system provider can reach a larger population of users. FEPs have been known to have a lower standard of security protection than the conventional systems to which they were attached.

## Viewdata standards
The UK viewdata standard — the particular graphics set and method of transmitting frames — is adopted in many other European countries and in former UK imperial possessions. Numbers and passwords to access these services occasionally appear on bulletin boards and the systems are particularly interesting to enter while they are still on trial. As a result of a quirk of Austrian law, anyone can legitimately enter their service without a password; though one is needed if you are to extract valuable information. However, important variants to the UK standards exist: the French (inevitably) have a system that is remarkably similar in outline but incompatible. In North America, the emerging standard which was originally put together by the Canadians for their Telidon service but which has now, with

modifications, been promoted by Ma Bell, has high resolution graphics because, instead of building up images from block graphics, it uses picture description techniques (eg draw line, draw arc, fill-in etc) of the sort relatively familiar to most users of modern home micros. Implementations of NALPS (as the US standard is called) are available for the IBM PC.

The Finnish public service uses software which can handle nearly all viewdata formats, including a near-photographic mode. Software similar to that used in the Finnish public service can be found on some private systems.

Countries vary considerably in their use of viewdata technology: the German and Dutch systems consist almost entirely of gateways to third-party computers; the French originally cost-justified their system by linking it to a massive project to make all telephone directories open to electronic enquiry, thus saving the cost of printed versions. French viewdata terminals thus have full alpha-keyboards instead of the numbers-only versions common in other countries. For the French, the telephone directory is central and all other information peripheral. Teletel/Antiope, as the service is called, suffered its first serious hack late in 1984 when a journalist on the political/satirical weekly *Le Canard Enchaine* claimed to have penetrated the Atomic Energy Commission's computer files accessible via Teletel and uncovered details of laser projects, nuclear tests in the South Pacific and an experimental nuclear reactor.

### Viewdata: the future

Viewdata grew up at a time when the idea of mass computer ownership was a fantasy, when the idea that private individuals could store and process data locally was considered far-fetched and when there were fears that the general public would have difficulties in tackling anything more complicated than a numbers-only key-pad. These failures of prediction have lead to the limitations and clumsiness of present-day viewdata. Nevertheless, the energy and success of the hardware salesmen plus the reluctance of companies and organisations to change their existing set-ups will ensure that for some time to come, new private viewdata systems will continue to be introduced...and be worth trying to break into.

There is one dirty trick that hackers have performed on private viewdata systems. Entering them is often easy, because high-level editing passwords are, as mentioned earlier, sometimes desperately insecure (see chapter 6) and it is easy to acquire editing status. Once you have discovered you are an editor, you can go to edit mode and edit the first page on the system, page 0: you can usually place your own message on it, of course; but you can also default all the routes to page 90. Now *90# in most viewdata systems is the log-out command, so the effect is that, as soon as someone logs in successfully and tries to go beyond the first page, the system logs them out....

However, this is no longer a new trick, and one which should be used with caution: is the database used by an important organisation? Are you going to tell the system manager what you have done and urge more care in password selection in future?

# CHAPTER 9

# Radio Computer Data

Vast quantities of data traffic are transmitted daily over the radio frequency spectrum; hacking is simply a matter of hooking up a good quality radio receiver and a computer through a suitable interface. On offer are news services from the world's great press agencies, commercial and maritime messages, meteorological data, and plenty of heavily-encrypted diplomatic and military traffic. A variety of systems, protocols and transmission methods are in use and the hacker jaded by land-line communication (and perhaps for the moment put off by the cost of phone calls) will find plenty of fun on the airwaves.

The techniques of radio hacking are similar to those necessary for computer hacking. Data transmission over the airwaves uses either a series of audio tones to indicate binary 0 and 1 which are modulated on transmit and demodulated on receive or alternatively frequency shift keying which involves the sending of one of two slightly different radio frequency carriers, corresponding to binary 0 or binary 1. The two methods of transmission sound identical on a communications receiver (see below) and both are treated the same for decoding purposes. The tones are different from those used on land-lines — 'space' is nearly always 1275 Hz and 'mark' can be one of three tones: 1445 Hz (170 Hz shift — quite often used by amateurs and with certain technical advantages); 1725 Hz (450 Hz shift — the one most commonly used by commercial and news services) and 2125 Hz (850 Hz shift — also used commercially). The commonest protocol uses the 5-bit Baudot code rather than 7-bit or 8-bit ASCII. The asynchronous, start/stop mode is the most common. Transmission speeds include: 45 baud (60 words/minute), 50 baud (66 words/minute), 75 baud (100 words/minute). 50 baud is the most common. However, many interesting variants can be heard — special versions of Baudot for non-European languages, error correction protocols, and various forms of facsimile.

The material of greatest interest is to be found in the high frequency or 'short wave' part of the radio spectrum, which goes from 2 MHz, just above the top of the medium wave broadcast band, through to 30 MHz, which is the far end of the 10-meter amateur band which itself is just above the well-known Citizens' Band at 27 MHz.

The reason this section of the spectrum is so interesting is that, unique among radio waves, it has the capacity for world-wide propagation without the use of satellites, the radio signals being bounced back, in varying degrees, by the ionosphere. This special quality means that *everyone* wants to use HF (high frequency) transmission — not only international broadcasters, the propaganda efforts of which are the most familiar uses of HF. Data transmission certainly occurs on all parts of the radio spectrum, from VLF (Very Low Frequency, the portion below the Long Wave broadcast band which is used for submarine communication), through the commercial and military VHF and UHF bands, beyond SHF (Super High Frequency, just above 1000 MHz) right to the microwave bands. But HF is the most rewarding in terms of range of material available, content of messages and effort required to access it.

Before going any further, hackers should be aware that in a number of countries even *receiving* radio traffic for which you are not licensed is an offence; in nearly all countries *making use* of information so received is also an offence and, in the case of news agency material, breach of copyright may also present a problem. However, owning the equipment required is usually not illegal and, since few countries require a special license to *listen* to amateur radio traffic (as opposed to transmitting, where a license is needed) and since amateurs transmit in a variety of data modes as well, hackers can set about acquiring the necessary capability without fear.

### Equipment
The equipment required consists of a communications receiver, an antenna, an interface unit/software and a computer.

*Communications receiver* This is the name given to a good quality high frequency receiver. Suitable models can be obtained, second-hand, at around £100; new receivers cost upwards of £175. There is no point is buying a radio simply designed to pick up shortwave broadcasts which will lack the sensitivity, selectivity and resolution necessary. A minimum specification would be:

| | |
|---|---|
| Coverage | 500 kHz — 30 MHz |
| Resolution | >100 Hz |

| Modes | AM, Upper Side Band, Lower Side Band, CW (Morse) |

Tuning would be either by two knobs, one for MHz, one for kHz, or by keypad. On more expensive models it is possible to vary the bandwidth of the receiver so that it can be widened for musical fidelity and narrowed when listening to bands with many signals close to one another.

Broadcast stations transmit using AM (amplitude modulation), but in the person-to-person contacts of the aeronautical, maritime and amateur world, single-side-band-suppressed carrier techniques are used — the receiver will feature a switch marked AM, USB, LSB, CW etc. Side-band transmission uses less frequency space and so allows more simultaneous conversations to take place, and is also more efficient in its use of the power available at the transmitter. The chief disadvantage is that equipment for receiving is more expensive and must be more accurately tuned. Upper side band is used on the whole for voice traffic, and lower side band for data traffic. (Radio amateurs are an exception: they also use lower side-band for voice transmissions below 10 MHz.)

Suitable sources of supply for communications receivers are amateur radio dealers, whose addresses may be found in specialist magazines like *Practical Wireless, Amateur Radio, Ham Radio Today*.

*Antenna* Antennas are crucial to good shortwave reception — the sort of short 'whip' aerial found on portable radios is quite insufficient if you are to capture transmissions from across the globe. When using a computer close to a radio you must also take considerable care to ensure that interference from the CPU and monitor don't squash the signal you are trying to receive. The sort of antenna I recommend is the 'active dipole', which has the twin advantages of being small and of requiring little operational attention. It consists of a couple of 1-meter lengths of wire tied parallel to the ground and meeting in a small plastic box. This is mounted as high as possible, away from interference, and is the 'active' part. From the plastic box descends coaxial cable which is brought down to a small power supply next to the receiver and from there the signal is fed into the receiver itself. The plastic box contains special low-noise transistors.

It is possible to use simple lengths of wire, but these usually operate well only on a limited range of frequencies, and you will need to cover the entire HF spectrum. Active antennas can be obtained by mail order from suppliers advertising in amateur radio magazines — the Datong is highly recommended.

*Interface* The 'interface' is the equivalent of the modem in landline communications; indeed, advertisements of newer products actually refer to radio modems. Radio tele-type, or RTTY, as it is called, is traditionally received on a modified teleprinter or telex machine; and the early interfaces or terminal units (TUs) simply converted the received audio tones into 'mark' and 'space' to act as the equivalent of the electrical line conditions of a telex circuit. Since the arrival of the microcomputer, however, the design has changed dramatically and the interface now has to perform the following functions:

1 Detect the designated audio tones

2 Convert them into electrical logic states

3 Strip the start/stop bits, convert the Baudot code into ASCII equivalents, reinsert start/stop bits

4 Deliver the new signal into an appropriate port on the computer. (If RS232C is not available, then any other port, e.g. game, that is)

A large number of designs exist: some consist of hardware interfaces plus a cassette, disc or ROM for the software; others contain both the hardware for signal acquisition and firmware for its decoding in one box.

Costs vary enormously and do not appear to be related to quality of result. The kit-builder with a ZX81 can have a complete set-up for under £40; semi-professional models, including keyboards and screen can cost in excess of £1000.

The kit I use is based on the Apple II (because of that model's great popularity in the USA, much hardware and software exists); the interface talks into the game port and I have several items of software to present Baudot, ASCII or Morse at will. There is even some interesting software for the Apple which needs no extra hardware — the audio from the receiver is fed direct into the cassette port of the Apple, but this method is difficult to replicate

102

on other machines because of the Apple's unique method of reading data from cassette.

Excellent inexpensive hard/firmware is available for many Tandy computers, and also for the VIC20/Commodore 64. On the whole US suppliers seem better than those in the UK or Japan — products are advertised in the US magazines *QST* and *73*.

*Setting Up* Particular attention should be paid to linking all the equipment together; there are special problems about using sensitive radio receiving equipment in close proximity to computers and VDUs. Computer logic blocks, power supplies and the synchronising pulses on VDUs are all excellent sources of radio interference (rfi). RFI appears not only as individual signals at specific points on the radio dial, but also as a generalised hash which can blank out all but the strongest signals.

Interference can escape from poorly packaged hardware, but also from unshielded cables which act as aerials. The remedy is simple to describe: encase and shield everything, connecting all shields to a good earth, preferably one separate from the mains earth. In practice, much attention must be paid to the detail of the interconnections and the relative placing of items of equipment. In particular, the radio's aerial should use coaxial feeder with a properly earthed outer braid, so that the actual wires that pluck the signals from the ether are well clear of computer-created rfi. It is always a good idea to provide a communications receiver with a proper earth, though it will work without one: if used with a computer, it is essential.

Do not let these paragraphs put you off; with care excellent results can be obtained. And bear in mind my own first experience: ever eager to try out some new kit, I banged everything together with great speed — ribbon cable, poor solder joints, an antenna taped quickly to a window in a metal frame less than two meters from the communications receiver — and all I could hear from 500 kHz to 30 MHz, wherever I tuned, was a great howl-whine of protest...

## Where to listen

Scanning through the bands on a good communications receiver, you realise just how crowded the radio spectrum is. The table in Appendix VI gives you an outline of the sandwich-like fashion in which the bands are organised.

The 'fixed' bands are the ones of interest; more particularly, the following ones are where you could expect to locate news agency transmissions (in kHz):

| | | | |
|---|---|---|---|
| 3155 | — | 3400 | |
| 3500 | — | 3900 | |
| 3950 | — | 4063 | |
| 4438 | — | 4650 | |
| 4750 | — | 4995 | |
| 5005 | — | 5480 | |
| 5730 | — | 5950 | |
| 6765 | — | 7000 | |
| 7300 | — | 8195 | |
| 9040 | — | 9500 | |
| 9900 | — | 9995 | |
| 10100 | — | 11175 | |
| 11400 | — | 11650 | |
| 12050 | — | 12330 | |
| 13360 | — | 13600 | |
| 13800 | — | 14000 | |

| | | |
|---|---|---|
| 14350 | — | 14990 |
| 15600 | — | 16360 |
| 17410 | — | 17550 |
| 18030 | — | 18068 |
| 18168 | — | 18780 |
| 18900 | — | 19680 |
| 19800 | — | 19990 |
| 20010 | — | 21000 |
| 21850 | — | 21870 |
| 22855 | — | 23200 |
| 23350 | — | 24890 |
| 25010 | — | 25070 |
| 25210 | — | 25550 |
| 26175 | — | 28000 |
| 29700 | — | 30005 |

In addition, amateurs tend to congregate around certain spots on the frequency map: 3590, 14090, 21090, 28090, and at VHF/UHF: 144.600, 145.300, MHz 432.600, 433.300.

**Tuning In**
Radio Teletype signals have a characteristic two-tone warble sound which you will hear properly only if your receiver is operating in SSB (single-side-band) mode. There are other digital tone-based signals to be heard: FAX (facsimile), Helschcrieber (which uses a technique similar to dot-matrix printers and is used for Chinese and related pictogram-style alphabets), SSTV (slow scan television, which can take up to 8 seconds to send a low-definition picture), and others.

But with practice, the particular sound of RTTY can easily be recognised. More experienced listeners can also identify shifts and speeds by ear.

You should tune into the signal watching the indicators on your terminal unit to see that the tones are being properly captured — typically, this involves getting two LEDs to flicker simultaneously. The software will now try to decode the signal, and it will be up to you to set the speed and 'sense'. The first speed to try is 66/7 words per minute, which corresponds to 50 baud, as this is the most common. On the amateur bands, the usual speed is 60 words per minute (45 baud); thereafter, if the rate sounds unusually fast, you try 100 words per minute (approximately 75 baud). By 'sense' or 'phase' is meant whether the higher tone corresponds to logical 1 or logical 0. Services can use either format; indeed the same transmission channel may use one 'sense' on one occasion and the reverse 'sense' on another. Your software can usually cope with this. If it can't, all is not lost: you retune your receiver to the opposite, side-band and the phase will thereby be reversed. So, if you are listening on the lower side-band (LSB), usually the conventional way to receive, you simply switch over to USB (upper side-band), retune the signal into the terminal unit, and the 'sense' will have been reversed.

Many news agency stations try to keep their channels open even if they have no news to put out: usually they do this by sending test messages like: 'The quick brown fox....' or sequences like 'RYRYRYRYRYRY...' such signals are useful for testing purposes, if a little dull to watch scrolling up the VDU screen.

You will discover many signals that you can't decode: the commonest reason is that the transmissions do not use European alphabets, and all the elements in the Baudot code have been re-assigned — some versions of Baudot use not one shift, but two, to give the required range of characters. Straightforward encrypted messages are usually recognisable as coming in groups of five letters, but the encryption can also operate at the bit- as well as at the character-level — in that case, too, you will get gobbleydegook.

A limited amount of ASCII code as opposed to Baudot is to be found, but mostly on the amateur bands.

Finally, an error-correction protocol, called SITOR, is increasingly to be found on the maritime bands, with AMTOR, an amateur variant, in the amateur bands. SITOR has various modes of operation but, in its fullest implementation, messages are sent in blocks which must be formally acknowledged by the recipient before the next one is despatched. The transmitter keeps trying until an acknowledgement is received. You may even come across, on the amateur bands, packet radio, which has some of the features of packet switching on digital land lines. This is one of the latest enthusiasms in amateur radio with at least two different protocols in relatively wide use. Discussion of SITOR and packet radio is beyond the scope of this book, but the reader is referred to BARTG (the British Amateur Radio Teletype Group) and its magazine *Datacom* for further information. You do not need to be a licensed radio amateur to join. The address is: 27 Cranmer Court, Richmond Road, Kingston KT2 5PY.

Operational problems of radio hacking are covered at the end of Appendix I, the Baudot code is given Appendix IV and an outline frequency plan is to be found in Appendix VI.

The material that follows represents some of the types of common transmissions: news services, test slips (essentially

devices for keeping a radio channel open), and amateur. The
corruption in places is due either to poor radio propagation
conditions or to the presence of interfering signals.


REVUE DE LA PRESSE ITALIENNE DU VENDREDI 28 DECEMBR
E 1984
;;;;;;;;;;;;;;;;;;;;;;;;;;;;;;;;;;;;;;;;;;;;;;;;;;;;;;;;;;;;;

   LE PROCES AUX ASSASSINS DE L-\\3 POIELUSZKO, LA VISITE DE
M. SPADOLINI A ISRAEL, LA SITUATION AU CAMBODGE ET LA GUER-
ILLA AU MOZAMBIQUE FONT LES TITES DES PAGES POLITIQUES


      MOBILISATION TO WORK FOR THE ACCOUNT OF 1985

             - AT THE ENVER HOXHA AUTOMOBILE AND
               TRACTOR COMBINE IN TIRANA 2

   TIRANA, JANUARY XATA/. - THE WORKING PEOPLE OF THE ENVER HOXHA
AUTOMOBILE AND TRACTOR COMBINE BEGAN THEIR WORK WITH VIGOUR
AND MOBILISATION FOR THE ACCOUNT OF 1985. THE WORK IN THIS
IMPROVOWNT CENTER FOR MECHANICAL INDUSTRY WAS NOT INTERRUPTED
FOR ONE MOMENT AND THE WORKING PEOPLE 83$ ONE ANOTHER FOR
FRESHER GREATER VICTORIES UNDER THE LEADERSHIP OF THE PARTY
WITH ENVER HOXHA AT THE HEAD, DURING THE SHIFTS, NEAR
THE FURNANCES, PRESSES ETC.. JUST LIKE SCORES OF WORKING COLLE-
CTIVES OF THE COUNTRY WHICH WERE NOT AT HOME DURING THE NEW
YEAR B
A
IN THE FRONTS OF WORK FOR THE BENEFITS OF THE SOCI-
ALIST CONSTRUCTION OF THE COUNTRY.
   PUTTING INTO LIFE THE TEACHINGS OF THE PARTY AND THE INSTRU-
CTIONS OF COMRADE ENVER HOXHA, THE WORKING COLLECTIVE OF THIS
COMBINE SCORED FRESH SUCCESSES DURING 1984 TO REALIZE THE
INDICES OF THE STATE PLAN BY RASING THE ECEONOMIC EFFECTIVE-
NESS. THE WORKING PEOPLE SUCCESSFULLY REALIZED AND OVERFUL
FILLED THE OBJECTIVE OF THE REVOLUTIONARY DRIVE ON THE HIGHER
EFFECTIOVENESS OF PRODUCTION, UNDERTAKEN IN KLAIDQAULSK SO,
WITHIN 1984 THE PLANNED PRODUCTIVITY, ACCORDING TO THE INDEX
OF THE FIVE YEAR PLAN, WAS OVERFULFILLED BY 2 PER CENT.
MOREOVER, THE FIVE YEAR PLAN FOR THE GMWERING OF THE COST OF
PRODUCTION WAS RAISED 2 MONTHS AHEAD OF TIME, ONE FIVE YEAR
PLAN FOR THE PRODUCTION OF MACHINERIES LAND EQUIPMENT AND
THE PRODUCTION OF THE TRACTORS WAS OVER-
FULFILLED. THE NET INCOME OF THE FIVE YEAR PLAN WAS REALIZED
WITHIN 4 YEARS. ETCM


RYRYRYRYRYRYRYRYRYRYRYRYRYRYRYRYRYRYRYRYRYRYRYRYRYRYRYRYRYRY
YRYRYRYRYRYRYRYRYRYRYRYRYRYRYRYRYRYRYRYRYRYRYRYRYRYRYRYRYRYR
RYRYRYRYRYRYRYRYRYRYRYRYRYRYRYRYRYRYRYRYRYRYRYRYRYRYRYRYRYRY
RYRYRYRYRYRYRYRYRYRYRYRYRYRYRYRYRYRYRYRYRYRYRYRYRYRYRYRYRYRY

RYRYRYRYRYRYRYRYRYRYRYRYRYRYRYRYRYRYRYRYRYRYRYRYD DE GJ4YAD
GJ4YAD GJ4YAD DE G4DF G4DF
SOME QRM BUT MOST OK. THE SHIFT IS NORMAL...SHIFT IS NORMAL.
FB ON YOUR RIG AND NICE TO MEET YOU IN RTTY. THE WEATHER HERE
TODAY IS FINE AND BEEN SUNNY BUT C9LD. I HAVE BEEN IN THIS MODE
BEFORE BUT NOT FOR A FEW YEARS HI HI.


GJ4YAD GJ4YAD DE G4DF G4DF
PSE KKK




G4EJE G4EJE DE G3IMS G3IMS
TNX FOR COMING BACK. RIG HERE IS ICOM 720A BUT I AM SENDING
AFSK NOT FSK. I USED TO HAVE A CREED BUT CHUCKED IT OUT IT WAS
TOO NOISY AND NOW HAVE VIC20 SYSTEM AND SOME US KIT MY SON
BROUGHT ME HE TRAVELS A LOT.
HAD LOTS OF TROUBLE WITH RFI AND HAVE NOT YET CURED IT. VERTY BAD
QRM AT MOMENT. CAN GET NOTHING ABOVE 10 MEGS AND NOT MUCH EX-G ON
80. HI HI. SUNSPOT COUNT IS REALLY LOW.

G4EJE G4EJE DE G3IMS G3IMS
KKKKKKKKKKK
RYRYRYRYRYRYRYRYRYR
KKKKKKKKKKK


G3IMS G3IMS DE G4EJE G4EJE
FB OM. QRM IS GETTING WORSE. I HAVE ALWAYS LIKED ICOM RIGS BUT
THEY ARE EXEPENSIVE. CAN YOU RUN FULL 100 PER CENT DUTY CYCLE ON
RTTY OR DO YOU HAVE TO RUN AROUND 50 PER CENT. I GET OVER-HEATING
ON THIS OLD YAESU 101. WHAT SORT OF ANTENNA SYSTEM DO YOU USE.
HERE IS A TRAPPED VERTICAL WITH 80 METERS TUNED TO RTTY SPOT AT
3590.
I STILL USE CREED 7 THOUGH AM GETTING FED UP WITH MECHANICAL
BREAK-DOWN AND NOISE BUT I HAVE HEARD ABOUT RFI AND HOME
COMPUTERS. MY NEPHEW HAS A SPECTRUM, CAN YOU GET RTTY SOFTWARE
FOR THAT/.

G3IMS G3IMS DE G4EJE G4EJE
PSE KKK

# CHAPTER 10

# Hacking: the Future

Security is now probably the biggest single growth area within the mainstream computer business. At conference after conference, consultants compete with each other to produce the most frightening statistics.

The main concern, however, is not hacking but fraud. Donn Parker, a frequent writer and speaker on computer crime based at the Stanford Research Institute has put US computer fraud at $3000 million a year; although reported crimes amount to only $100 million annually. In June 1983 the *Daily Telegraph* claimed that British computer-related frauds could be anything between £500 million and £2.5 billion a year. Detective Inspector Ken McPherson, head of the computer crime unit at the Metropolitan Police, was quoted in 1983 as saying that within 15 years every fraud would involve a computer. The trouble is, very few victims are prepared to acknowledge their losses. To date, no British clearing bank has admitted to suffering from an out-and-out computer fraud, other than the doctoring of credit and plastic ID cards. Few consultants believe that they have been immune.

However, to put the various threats in perspective, here are two recent US assessments. Robert P Campbell of Advanced Information Management, formerly head of computer security in the US Army, reckons that only one computer crime in 100 is detected; of those detected, 15 per cent or fewer are reported to the authorities, and that of those reported, one in 33 is successfully prosecuted — a 'clear-up' rate of one in 22,000.

And Robert Courtney, former security chief at IBM produced a list of hazards to computers: 'The No 1 problem now and forever is errors and omissions'. Then there is crime by insiders, particularly non-technical people of three types: single women under 35; 'little old ladies' over 50 who want to give the money to charity; and older men who feel their careers have left them neglected. Next, natural disasters. Sabotage by disgruntled employees. Water damage. As for hackers and other outsiders who break in, he estimates it is less than 3 per cent of the total.

Here in the UK, the National Computing Centre says that at least 90 per cent of computer crimes involve putting false information into a computer, as opposed to sophisticated logic techniques; such crimes are identical to conventional embezzlement: looking for weaknesses in an accounting system and taking advantage. In such cases the computer merely carries out the fraud with more thoroughness than a human, and the print-out gives the accounts a spurious air of being correct.

In the meantime, we are on the threshold of a new age of opportunities for the hacker. The technology we can afford has suddenly become much more interesting.

The most recent new free magazines to which I have acquired subscriptions are for owners of the IBM PC, its variants and clones. There are two UK monthlies for regular users, another for corporate buyers and several US titles.

The IBM PC is only partly aimed at small business users as a stand-alone machine to run accounting, word processing, spreadsheet calculation and the usual business dross; increasingly the marketing is pitching it as an executive work-station, so that the corporate employee can carry out functions not only local to his own office, but can access the corporate mainframe as well — for data, messaging with colleagues, and for greater processing power.

In page after page, the articles debate the future of this development — do employees *want* work-stations? Don't many bosses still feel that anything to do with typing is best left to their secretary? How does the executive workstation relate to the mainframe? Do you allow the executive to merely *collect* data from it, or input as well? If you permit the latter, what effect will this have on the integrity of the mainframe's files? How do you control what is going on? What is the future of the DP professional? Who is in charge?

And so the articles go on. Is IBM about to offer packages which integrate mainframes and PCs in one enormous system, thus effectively blocking out every other computer manufacturer and software publisher in the world by sheer weight and presence?

I don't know the answers to these questions, but elsewhere in these same magazines is evidence that the hardware products to support the executive workstation revolution are there — or, even if one has the usual cynicism about computer trade advertising ahead of actual availability, about to be.

The products are high quality terminal emulators, not the sort of thing hitherto achieved in software — variants on asynchronous protocols with some fancy cursor addressing — but cards capable of supporting a variety of key synchronous communications, like 327x (bisynch and SDLC), and handling high-speed file transfers in CICs, TSO, IMS and CMS. These products feature special facilities, like windowing or replicate aspects of mainframe operating systems like VM (Virtual Machine), giving the user the experience of having several different computers simultaneously at his command. Other cards can handle IBM's smaller mini-mainframes, the Systems/34 and /38. Nor are other mainframe manufacturers with odd-ball comms requirements ignored: ICL, Honeywell and Burroughs are all catered for. There are even several PC add-ons which give a machine direct X.25; it can sit on a packet-switched network without the aid of a PAD.

Such products are expensive by personal micro standards, but it means that, for the expenditure of around £8000, the hacker can call up formidable power from his machine. The addition of special environments on these new super micros which give the owner direct experience of mainframe operating systems — and the manuals to go with them — will greatly increase the population of knowledgeable computer buffs. Add to this the fact that the corporate workstation market, if it is at all succesful, must mean that many executives will want to call their mainframe from home — and there will be many many more computer ports on the PTSN or sitting on PSS.

There can be little doubt that the need for system security will play an increasing role in the specification of new mainframe installations. For some time, hardware and software engineers have had available the technical devices necessary to make a computer secure; the difficulty is to get regular users to implement the appropriate methods — humans can only memorise a limited number of passwords. I expect greater use will be made of threat monitoring techniques: checking for sequences of unsuccessful attempts at logging in, and monitoring the level of usage of customers for extent, timing, and which terminals or ports they appear on.

The interesting thing as far as hackers are concerned is that it is the difficulty of the exercise that motivates us, rather than the prospect of instant wealth. It is also the flavour of naughty, but not outright, illegality. I remember the Citizens Band radio boom of a few years ago: it started quietly with just a handful of London breakers who had imported US sets, really simply to talk to a few friends. One day everyone woke up, switched on their rigs and discovered overnight there was a whole new sub-culture out there, breathing the ether. Every day there were more and more until no spare channels could be found. Then some talented engineers found out how to freak the rigs and add another 40 channels to the original 40. And then another 40. Suddenly there were wholesalers and retailers and fanzines, all selling and promoting products the using or manufacturing of which was illegal under British law.

Finally, the government introduced a legalised CB, using different standards from the imported US ones. Within six months the illegal scene had greatly contracted, and no legal CB service of comparable size ever took its place. Manufacturers and shop-keepers who had expected to make a financial killing were left with warehouses full of the stuff. Much of the attraction of AM CB was that it was forbidden and unregulated. There is the desire to be an outlaw, but clever and not too outrageous with it, in very many of us.

So I don't believe that hacking can be stopped by tougher security, or by legislation, or even by the fear of punishment. Don't get me wrong: I regard computers as vastly beneficial. But they can threaten our traditional concepts of freedom, individuality and human worth I like to believe hacking is a curious re-assertion of some of those ideas.

The challenge of hacking is deeply ingrained in many computer enthusiasts; where else can you find an activity the horizons of which are constantly expanding, where new challenges and dangers can be found every day, where you are not playing a visibly artificial 'game', where so much can be accessed with so little resource but a small keyboard, a glowing VDU, an inquisitive and acquisitive brain, and an impish mentality?

# Trouble Shooting

The assumption is that you are operating in the default mode of 300/300 baud asynchronous using CCITT tones, 7 bits, even parity, one stop bit, full-duplex/echo off, originate. You have dialled the remote number, seized the line and can hear a data tone. Something is not working properly. This is a partial list of possibilities.

*The screen remains blank*
- A physical link has failed — check the cables between computer, modem and phone line.
- The remote modem needs waking up — send a <cr> or failing that, a ENQ (<ctrl>E), character.
- The remote modem is operating at a different speed. Some modems can be brought up to speed by hitting successive <cr>s; they usually begin at 110 baud and then go to 300, so two successive <cr>s should do the trick.
- The remote modem is not working at V21 standards, either because it is a different CCITT standard, e.g. V22, V22 bis, V23 etc or operates on Bell (US) tones. Since different standards tend to have different 'wake-up' tones which are easily recognised with practice, you may be able to spot what is happening. It shouldn't need to be said that if you are calling a North American service you should assume Bell tones.
- Both your modem and that of the remote service are in answer or in originate and so cannot 'speak' to each other. Always assume you are in the originate mode.
- The remote service is not using ASCII/International Alphabet No 5.

*The screen fills with random characters*
- Data format different from your defaults — check 7 or 8 bit characters, even/odd parity, stop and start bits.
- Mismatch of characters owing to misdefined protocol — check start/stop, try alternately EOB/ACK and XON/XOF.
- Remote computer operating at a different speed from you — try, in order, 110, 300, 600, 1200, 75.

- Poor physical connection — if using an acoustic coupler check location of handset, if not, listen on line to see if it is noisy or crossed.
- The remote service is not using ASCII/International Alphabet No 5.

*Every character appears twice*
- You are actually in half-duplex mode and the remote computer as well as your own are both sending characters to your screen — switch to full-duplex/echo off.

*All information appears on only one line, which is constantly overwritten*
- The remote service is not sending line feeds — if your terminal software has the facility, enable it to induce line feeds when each display line is filled. Many on-line services and public dial-up ports let you configure the remote port to send line feeds and vary line length. Your software may have a facility to show control characters, in which case you will see <ctrl>J if the remote service is sending line feeds.

*Wide spaces appear between display lines*
- The remote service is sending line feeds and your software is inducing another one simultaneously — turn off your induced carriage return facility. In 'show control character' mode, you will see <ctrl>Js.

*Display lines are broken awkwardly*
- The remote service is expecting your screen to support more characters than it is able. Professional services tend to expect 80 characters across whilst many personal computers may have less than 40, so that they can be read on a tv screen. Check if your software can help, but you may have to live with it. Alternatively, the remote computer may let you reconfigure its character stream.

*Most of the display makes sense, but every so often it becomes garbled*
- You have intermittent line noise — check if you can command the remote computer to send the same stream again and see if you get the garbling.
- The remote service is sending graphics instructions which your computer and software can't resolve.

*The display contains recognisable characters in definite groupings, but otherwise makes no sense*
- The data is intended for an intelligent terminal, which will combine the transmitted data with a local program so that it makes sense.
- The data is intended for batch processing.
- The data is encrypted

*Although the stream of data appeared properly on your vdu, when you try to print it out, you get corruption and over-printing*
- Most printers use a series of special control characters to enable various functions — line feeds, back-space, double-intensity, special graphics etc. The remote service is sending a series of control characters which, though not displayed on your screen, are 'recognised' by your printer, though often in not very helpful ways. You may be able to correct the worst problems in software, e.g. by enabling line-feeds; alternatively many printers can be re-configured in hardware by appropriate settings of DIL switches internally.

*When accessing a viewdata service, the screen fills with squares.* The square is the standard display default if your viewdata terminal can't make sense of the data being sent to it.
- Check physical connections and listen for line noise.
- The viewdata host does not work to UK viewdata standards — French viewdata uses parallel attributes and has a number of extra features. The CEPT standard for Europe contains features from both the UK and French systems and you may be able to recognise some of the display. North American videotex is alpha-geometric and sends line drawing instructions rather than characters.
- The viewdata host has enhanced graphics features, perhaps for dynamically redefined character sets, alphageometric instructions, or alpha-photographic (full resolution) pictures. If the host has some UK standard-compatible features, you will be able to read them normally. If the cursor jumps about the screen, the host has dynamic graphics facilities. If the viewdata protocol is anything at all like the UK standard, you should see regular clear-screens as each new page comes up; however, advanced graphics features tend to work by suppressing clear-screens.
- The service you have dialled is not using viewdata. PSS is accessible at 75/1200, as are one or two direct-dial services. In this case you should be seeing a conventional display or trying

one of the other suggestions in this appendix. It is usual to assume that any subscriber dialling into a 75/1200 port has only a 40 character display.

*You can't see what you are typing*
- The remote computer is not echoing back to you — switch to half-duplex. If the remote computer's messages now appear doubled; that would be unusual but not unique; you will have to toggle back to full-duplex for receive.

*Data seems to come from the remote computer in jerky bursts rather than as a smooth stream*
- If you are using PSS or a similar packet-switched service and it is near peak business hours either in your time zone or in that of the host you are accessing, the effect is due to heavy packet traffic. There is nothing you can do — do not send extra commands to 'speed things up' as those commands will arrive at the host eventually and cause unexpected results.
- The host is pausing for a EOB/ACK or XON/XOF message — check your protocol settings — try sending ctrl-Q or ctrl-F.

*You have an apparently valid password but it is not accepted*
- You don't have a valid password, or you don't have all of it.
- The password has hidden control characters which don't display on the screen. Watch out for <ctrl>H — the back-space, which will over-write an existing displayed character.
- The password contains characters which your computer doesn't normally generate — check your terminal software and see if there is a way of sending them.

*Most of the time everything works smoothly, but you can't get past certain prompts*
- The remote service is looking for characters your computer doesn't normally generate. Check your terminal software and see if there is a way of sending them.

*A list or file called up turns out to be boring — can you stop it?*
- Try sending <ctrl>S; this may simply make the remote machine pause, until a <ctrl>Q is sent — and you may find the list resumes where it left off. On the other hand it may take you on to a menu.
- Send a BREAK signal (<ctrl>1). If one BREAK doesn't work, send another in quick succession.

*You wish to get into the operating system from an applications program.*

Don't we all? There is no standard way of doing this, and indeed it might be almost impossible, because the operating system can only be addressed by a few privileged terminals, of which yours (and its associated password) is not one. However, you could try the following:

- Immediately after signing on, send two BREAKs (<ctrl>1).
- Immediately after signing on, try combinations of ESC, CTRL and SHIFT. As a desperate measure, send two line feeds before signing on — this has been known to work!.
- At an options page, try requesting SYSTEM or some obvious contraction like SYS or X. If in the Basic language, depending on the dialect, SYSTEM or X in immediate mode should get you the operating system.

*You are trying to capture data traffic from a short-wave radio and are having little success*

- Your computer could be emitting so much radio noise itself that any signal you are attempting to hear is squashed. To test: tune your radio to a fairly quiet short-wave broadcast and then experiment listening to the background hash with the computer switched first on, then off. If the noise level drops when you turn off the computer, then you need to arrange for more rf suppression and to move the computer and radio further apart. Another source of rf noise is the sync scan in a tv tube.
- If you can hear the two-tones of rtty traffic but can't get letters resolved, check that your terminal unit is locking on to the signal (often indicated by LEDs); you should then at least get some response on your screen, if it doesn't make immediate sense.
- Once you have letters on screen, try altering the speed at which you are receiving (see chapter 10); check also that you are reading in the right 'sense', ie that mark and space have not been reversed.
- In addition to signals sent with the conventional International Telegraphic Code No 2 (Baudot), variants exist for foreign letter sets, like Cyrillic, which your software may not be able to resolve.
- There are other data-type services which sound a little like RTTY, but are not: they include FAX (facsimile) hellschreiber ( a form of remote dot-matrix printing), SITOR (see chapter 10) and special military/diplomatic systems.

# Glossary

This glossary collects together the sort of name, word, abbreviation phrase you could come across during your network adventures and for which you may not be able to find a precise definition

**ACK**
Non–printing character used in some comms protocols to indicate that a block has been received and that more can be sent; used in association with EOB.

**ANSI**
American National Standards Institute — one of a number of standards organizations.

**Answer mode**
When a modem is set up to receive calls — the usual mode for a host. The user's computer will be in originate.

**ARQ**
Automatic Repeat Request — method of error correction.

**ASCII**
American Standard Code for Information Interchange — alternate name for International Telegraph Alphabet No 5: 7-bit code to symbolise common characters and comms instructions, usually transmitted as 8-bit code to include a parity bit.

**ASR**
Automatic Send Receive — any keyboard terminal capable of generating a message into off-line storage for later transmission; includes paper-tape telex machines as well as microcomputers.

**Asynchronous**
Description of communications which rely on 'start' and 'stop' bits to synchronise originator and receiver of data — hence asynchrnous protocols, channels, modems, terminals etc.

**Backward channel**
Supervisory channel, not used as main channel of communication; in viewdata the 75 baud back from the user to the host.

**Baud**
Measure of the signalling rate on a data channel, number of signalling elements per second.

**Baseband**
Modulation is direct on the comms line rather than using audio or radio frequencies; used in some local area networks. A baseband or 'short-haul' modem can be used to link computers in adjacent offices, but not over telephone lines.

**Baudot**
5-bit data code used in telegraphy, telex and RTTY — also known as International Telegraph Alphabet No 2.

**Bell**
(1) non-printing character which sounds a bell or bleep, usually enabled by <ctrl> G; (2) Common name for US phone company and, in this context, specifiers for a number of data standards and services, e.g. Bell 103a, 202a, 212a, etc — see Appendix V

**Bit Binary digit**
value 0 or 1.

**Broadband**
Broadband data channels have a wider bandwidth than ordinary telephone circuits — 12 times in fact, to give a bandwidth of 48kHz, over which may simultaneous high-speed data transfers can take place.

**Broadcast service**
Data service in which all users receive the same information simultaneously, without the opportunity to interrogate or query; e.g. news services like AP, Reuters News, UPI etc. *See also* on-line service.

**Bisynchronous**
IBM protocol involving synchronous transmission of binary coded data.

**BLAISE**
British Library Automated Information Service — substantial bibliographic on-line host.

**BREAK**
Non-printing character used in some data transmission protocols and found on some terminals — can often be regenerated by using <ctrl>1.

**BSC**
Binary Synchronous Communications — see bisynchronous.

**Byte**
Group of bits (8) representing one data character.

**Call accept**
In packet-switching, the packet that confirms the party is willing to proceed with the call.

**Call redirection**
In packet-switching, allows call to be automatically redirected from original address to another, nominated address.

**Call request**
In packet-switching, packet sent to initiate a datacall.

**CCITT**
Comité Consultatif International Téléphonique et Télégraphique — committee of International Telecommunications Union which sets international comms standards. Only the US fails to follow its recommendations in terms of modem tones, preferring 'Bell' tones. The CCITT also sets such standards as V21, 24, X25 etc.

**Character terminal**
In packet-switching, a terminal which can only access via a PAD.

**Cluster**
When two or more terminals are connected to a data channel at a single point.

**Common Carrier**
A telecommunications resource providing facilities to the public.

**Connect-time**
Length of time connected to a remote computer, often the measure of payment. Contrast with cpu time or cpu units, which measures how much 'effort' the host put into the communication.

**CPS**
Characters Per Second.

**Cpu Time**
In an on-line session, the amount of time the central processor actually spends on the interaction process, as opposed to connect-time; either can be used as the basis of tariffing.

**CRC**
Cyclic Redundancy Check — error detection method.

**CUG**
Closed User Group — group of users/terminals who enjoy privacy with respect to a public service.

**Datacall**
In packet-switching, an ordinary call, sometimes called a 'switched virtual call'.

**Dataline**
In packet-switching, dedicated line between customer's terminal and packet-switch exchange (PSE).

**DCE**
Data Circuit-terminating Equipment — officialese for modems.

**DTE**
Data Terminal Equipment — officialese for computers.

**EBCDIC**
Extended Binary Coded Decimal Interchange Code — IBM's alternative to ASCII, based on an 8-bit code, usually transmitted synchronously. 256 characters are available.

**Emulator**
Software/hardware set-up which makes one device mimic another, e.g. a personal computer may emulate an industry-standard dumb terminal like the VT100. Compare simulator, which gives a device the attributes of another, but not necessarily in real time, e.g.

when a large mini carries a program making it simulate another computer to develop software.

**Euronet-Diane**
European direct access information network.

**Datel**
BT's name for its data services, covering both the equipment and the type of line, e.g. Datel 100 corresponds to telegraph circuits, Datel 200 is the usual 300/300 asynchronous service, Datel 400 is for one-way transmissions e.g. monitoring of remote sites, Datel 600 is a two- or four-wire asynchronous service at up to 1200 baud, Datel 2400 typically uses a 4-wire private circuit at 2400 baud synchronous, etc. etc.

**DES**
Data Encryption Standard — a US-approved method of encrypting data traffic, and somewhat controversial in its effectiveness.

**Dialog**
Well-established on-line host available world-wide covering an extensive range of scientific, bibiographic and news services. Also known as Lockheed Dialog.

**Dial-up**
Call initiated via PTSN, no matter where it goes after that; as opposed to service available via permanent leased line.

**Duplex**
Transmission in two directions simultaneously, sometimes called full-duplex; contrast half-duplex, in which alternate transmissions by either end are required. NB this is terminology used in data communications over land-lines. Just to confuse matters, radio technology refers to simplex, when only one party can transmit at a time and a single radio frequency is used; two-frequency-simplex or half-duplex when only one party can speak but two frequencies are used, as in repeater and remote base working; and full-duplex, when both parties can speak simultaneously and two radio frequencies are used, as in radio-telephones.

**Echo**
(1) When a remote computer sends back to the terminal each letter as it is sent to it for confirming re-display locally. (2) Effect on long comms lines caused by successive amplifications —

echo-suppressors are introduced to prevent disturbance caused by this phenomenon, but in some data transmission the echo-suppressors must be switched off.

**EIA**
Electronic Industries Association, US standards body.

**ENQ**
Non-printing character signifying 'who are you?' and often sent by hosts as they are dialled up. When the user's terminal receives ENQ it may be programmed to send out a password automatically. Corresponds to <esc> E.

**EOB**
End Of Block — non-printing character used in some protocols, usually in association with ACK.

**Equalisation**
Method of compensation for distortion over long comms channels.

**FDM**
Frequency Division Multiplexing — a wide bandwidth transmission medium, e.g. coaxial cable, supports several narrow bandwidth channels by differentiating by frequency; compare time division multiplexing.

**FSK**
Frequency Shift Keying — a simple signalling method in which frequencies but not phase or amplitude are varied according to whether '1' or '0' is sent — used in low-speed asynchronous comms both over land-line and by radio.

**Handshaking**
Hardware and software rules for remote devices to communicate with each other, supervisory signals such as 'wait', 'acknowledge', 'transmit', 'ready to receive' etc.

**HDLC**
In packet-switching, High Level Data Link Control procedure, an international standard which detects and corrects errors in the stream of data between the terminal and the exchange — and to provide flow control.

**Host**
The 'big' computer holding the information the user wishes to retrieve.

**Infoline**
Scientific on-line service from Pergamon.

**ISB**
*see* sideband.

**ISO**
International Standards Organisation.

**LAN**
Local Area Network — normally using coaxial cable, this form of network operates at high speed over an office or works site, but no further. May have inter-connect facility to PTSN or PSS.

**LF**
Line Feed — cursor moves active position down one line — usual code is <ctrl>J; not the same as carriage return, which merely sends cursor to left-hand side of line it already occupies. However, in many protocols/terminals/set-ups, hitting the <ret> or <enter> button means both <lf> and <cr>.

**Logical Channel**
Apparently continuous path from one terminal to another.

**LSB**
*see* sideband.

**KSR**
Keyboard Send Receive — terminal with keyboard on which anything that is typed is immediately sent. No off-line preparation facility, e.g. teletypewriter, 'dumb' terminals.

**Macro software**
Facility frequently found in comms programs which permits the preparation and sending of commonly-used strings of information, particularly passwords and routing instructions.

**Mark**
One of the two conditions on a data communications line, the other being 'space'; mark indicates 'idle' and is used as a stop bit.

**Message switching**
When a complete message is stored and then forwarded, as opposed to a packet of information. This technique is used in some electronic mail services, but not for general data transmission.

**Modem**
Modulator-demodulator.

**Multiplexer**
Device which divides a data channel into two or more independent channels.

**MVS**
Multiple Virtual Storage — IBM operating system dating from mid-70s.

**NUA**
Network User Address, number by which each terminal on a packet-switch network is identified (character terminals don't have them individually, because they use a PAD). In PSS, it's a 10-digit number.

**NUI**
Network User Identity, used in PSS for dial-up access by each user.

**Octet**
In packet-switching, 8 consecutive bits of user data, e.g. 1 character.

**On-line service**
Interrogative or query service available for dial-up. Examples include Lockheed Dialog, Blaise, Dow Jones News Retrieval, etc; leased-line examples include Reuters Monitor, Telerate.

**Originate**
Mode-setting for a modem operated by a user about to call another computer.

**OSI**
Open Systems Interconnect — intended world standard for digital network connections — c.f. SNA.

**Packet terminal**
Terminal capable of creating and disassembling packets, interacting with a packet-network, c.f. character terminal.

**PAD**
Packet Assembly/disassembly Device — permits 'ordinary' terminals to connect to packet switch services by providing addressing, headers, (and removal), protocol conversion etc.

**Parity checking**
Technique of error correction in which one bit is added to each data character so that the number of bits is always even (or always odd).

**PDP/8 & /11**
Large family of minis, commercially very sucessful, made by DEC. the PDP 8 was 12-bit, the PDP 11 is 16-bit. The LSI 11 have strong family connections to the PDP 11, as have some configurations of the desk-top Rainbow.

**Polling**
Method of controlling terminals on a clustered data network, where each is called in turn by the computer to see if it wishes to transmit or receive.

**Protocol**
Agreed set of rules.

**PSE**
Packet Switch Exchange — enables packet switching in a network.

**PTSN**
Public Switched Telephone Network — the voice-grade telephone network dialled from a phone. Contrast with leased lines, digital networks, conditioned lines etc.

**PTT**
jargon for the publicly-owned telecommunications authority/ utility

**PVC**
Permanent Virtual Circuit — a connection in packet switching which is always open, no set-up required.

**Redundancy checking**
Method of error correction.

**RS232C**
The list of definitions for interchange circuit: the US term for CCITT V24 — see Appendix III.

**RSX-11**
Popular operating system for PDP/11 family.

**RTTY**
Radio Teletype — method of sending telegraphy over radio waves.

**RUBOUT**
Back-space deleting character, using <ctrl>H.

**Secondary channel**
Data channel, usually used for supervision, using same physical path as main channel; in V23 which is usually 600 or 1200 baud half-duplex, 75 baud traffic is supervisory but in viewdata is the channel back from the user to the host, thus giving low-cost full duplex.

**Segment**
Chargeable unit of volume on PSS.

**Serial transmission**
One bit at a time, using a single pair of wires, as opposed to parallel transmission, in which several bits are sent simultaneously over a ribbon cable. A serial interface often uses many more than two wires between computer and modem or computer and printer, but only two wires carry the data traffic, the remainder being used for supervision, electrical power and earthing, or not at all.

**Sideband**
In radio the technique of suppressing the main carrier and limiting the transmission to the information-bearing sideband. To listen at the receiver, the carrier is re-created locally. The technique, which produces large economies in channel occupany, is extensively used in professional, non-broadcast applications. The full name is single side-band, supressed carrier. Each full carrier supports two sidebands, an upper and lower, USB and LSB respectively; in general, USB is used for speech, LSB for data, but this is only a

convention — amateurs used LSB for speech below 10 MHz, for example. ISB, independent side-band, is when the one carrier supports two sidebands with separate information on them, usually speech on one and data on the other. If you listen to radio teletype on the 'wrong' sideband, 'mark' and 'space' values become reversed with a consequent loss of meaning.

## SITOR
Error-correction protocol for sending data over radio-path using frequent checks and acknowledgements.

## SNA
System Network Architecture — IBM proprietary networking protocol, the rival to OSI.

## Space
One of two binary conditions in a data transmission channel, the other being 'mark'. Space is binary 0.

## Spooling
Simultaneous Peripheral Operation On-Line — more usually, the ability, while accessing a database, to store all fetched information in a local memory buffer, from which it may be recalled for later examination, or dumped to disc or printer.

## Start/Stop
Asynchronous transmission; the 'start' and 'stop' bits bracket each data character.

## Statistical Multiplexer
A statmux is an advanced multiplexer which divides one physical link between several data channels, taking advantage of the fact that not all channels bear equal traffic loads.

## STX
Start Text — non-printing character used in some protocols.

## SVC
Switched Virtual Circuit — in packet switching, when connection between two computers or computer and terminal must be set up by a specific call.

**SYN**
Non-printing character often used in synchronous transmission to tell a remote device to start its local timing mechanism.

**Synchronous**
Data transmission in which timing information is super-imposed on pure data. Under this method 'start/stop' techniques are not used and data exhange is more efficient, hence synchronous channel, modem, terminal, protocol etc.

**TDM**
Time Division Multiplex — technique for sharing several data channels along one high-grade physical link. Not as efficient as statistical techniques.

**Telenet**
US packet-switch common carrier.

**Teletex**
High-speed replacement for telex, as yet to find much commercial support.

**Teletext**
Use of vertical blanking interval in broadcast television to transmit magazines of text information, e.g. BBC's Ceefax and IBA's Oracle.

**Telex**
Public switched low-speed telegraph network.

**TOPIC**
The Stock Exchange's market price display service; it comes down a leased line and has some of the qualities of both viewdata and teletext.

**Tymnet**
US packet-switch common carrier.

**V-standards**
Set of recommendations by CCITT — see Appendix III.

**VAX**
Super-mini family made by DEC; often uses Unix operating system.

**Viewdata**

Technology allowing large numbers of users to access data easily on terminal based (originally) on modified tv sets. Information is presented in 'page' format rather than on a scrolling screen and the user issues all commands on a numbers-only keypad. Various standards exist of which the UK one is so far dominant; others include the European CEPT standard which is similar to the UK one, a French version and the US Presentation Level Protocol. Transmission speeds are usually 1200 baud from the host and 75 baud from the user. Viewdata together with teletext is known jointly as videotex(t).

**Virtual**

In the present context, a virtual drive, store, machine etc is one which appears to the user to exist, but is merely an illusion generated on a computer; thus several users of IBM's VM operating system each think they have an entire separate computer, complete with drives, discs and other peripherals — in fact the one actual machine can support several lower-level operating systems simultaneously.

**VT52/100**

Industry-standard general purpose computer terminals with no storage capacity or processing power but with the ability to be locally programmed to accept a variety of asynchronous transmission protocols — manufactured by DEC. The series has developed since the VT100.

**X-standards**

Set of recommendations by CCITT — see Appendix III.

**XON/XOF**

Pair of non-printing characters sometimes used in protocols to tell devices when to start or stop sending. XON often corresponds to <ctrl>Q and XOF to <ctrl>S.

**80-80**

Type of circuit used for telex and telegraphy — mark and space are indicated by conditions of — or + 80 volts. Also known in the UK as Tariff J. Usual telex speed is 50 baud, private wire telegraphy (news agencies etc) 75 baud.

# Selected CCITT Recommendations

**V series: Data transmission over telephone circuits**

| | |
|---|---|
| V1 | Power levels for data transmission over telephone lines |
| V3 | International Alphabet No 5 (ASCII) |
| V4 | General structure of signals of IA5 code for data transmission over public telephone network |
| V5 | Standardisation of modulation rates and data signalling rates for synchronous transmission in general switched network |
| V6 | Ditto, on leased circuits |
| V13 | Answerback simulator |
| V15 | Use of acoustic coupling for data transmission |
| V19 | Modems for parallel data transmission using telephone signalling frequencies |
| V20 | Parallel data transmission modems standardised for universal use in the general switched telephone network |
| V21 | 200 baud modem standardised |
| V22 | 1200 bps full-duplex 2-wire modem for PTSN |
| V22 bis | 2400 bps full-duplex 2-wire modem for PTSN |
| V23 | 600/1200 bps modem for PTSN |
| V24 | List of definitions for interchange circuits between data terminal equipment and data circuit-terminating equipment |
| V25 | Automatic calling and/or answering equipment on PTSN |
| V26 | 2400 bps modem on 4-wire circuit |
| V26 bis | 2400/1200 bps modem for PTSN |
| V27 | 4800 bps modem for leased circuits |
| V27 bis | 4800 bps modem (equalised) for leased circuits |
| V27 ter | 4800 bps modem for PTSN |
| V29 | 9600 bps modem for leased circuits |
| V35 | Data transmission at 48 kbits/sec using 60-108 kHz band circuits |

## X series: recommendations covering data networks

| | |
|---|---|
| X1 | International user classes of services in public data networks |
| X2 | International user facilities in public data networks |
| X3 | Packet assembly/disassembly facility (PAD) |
| X4 | General structure of signals of IA5 code for transmission over public data networks |
| X20 | Interface between data terminal equipment and data circuit-terminating equipment for start-stop transmission services on public data networks |
| X20 bis | V21—compatible interface |
| X21 | Interface for synchronous operation |
| X25 | Interface between data terminal equipment and data circuit-terminating equipment for terminals operating in the packet-switch mode on public data networks |
| X28 | DTE/DCE interface for start/stop mode terminal equipment accessing a PAD on a public data network |
| X29 | Procedures for exchange of control information and user data between a packet mode DTE and a PAD |
| X95 | Network parameters in public data networks |
| X96 | Call progress signals in public data networks |
| X121 | International addressing scheme for PDNs |

# Computer Alphabets

Four alphabets are in common use for computer communications: ASCII, also known as International Telegraphic Alphabet No 5; Baudot, used in telex and also known as International Telegraphic Alphabet No 2; UK Standard videotex, a variant of ASCII; and EDCDIC, used by IBM.

## ASCII

This is the standard, fully implemented character set. There are a number of national variants: # in the US variant is £ in the UK variant. Many micro keyboards cannot generate all the characters directly, particularly the non-printing characters used for control of transmission, effectors of format and information separators. The 'keyboard' column gives the usual method of providing them, but you should check the firmware/software manuals for your particular set-up. You should also know that many of the 'spare' control characters are often used to enable special features on printers.

| HEX | DEC | ASCII | Name | Keyboard | Notes |
|-----|-----|-------|------|----------|-------|
| 00 | 0 | NUL | Null | ctrl @ | |
| 01 | 1 | SOH | Start heading | ctrl A | |
| 02 | 2 | STX | Start text | ctrl B | |
| 03 | 3 | ETX | End text | ctrl C | |
| 04 | 4 | EOT | End transmission | ctrl D | |
| 05 | 5 | ENQ | Enquire | ctrl E | |
| 06 | 6 | ACK | Acknowledge | ctrl F | |
| 07 | 7 | BEL | Bell | ctrl G | |
| 08 | 8 | BS | Backspace | ctrl H | or special key |
| 09 | 9 | HT | Horizontal tab | ctrl I | or special key |
| 0A | 10 | LF | Line feed | ctrl J | |
| 0B | 11 | VT | Vertical tab | ctrl K | |
| 0C | 12 | FF | Form feed | ctrl L | |

| HEX | DEC | ASCII | Name | Keyboard | Notes |
|-----|-----|-------|------|----------|-------|
| 0D | 13 | CR | Carriage return | ctrl M | or special key |
| 0E | 14 | SO | Shift out | ctrl N | |
| 0F | 15 | SI | Shift in | ctrl O | |
| 10 | 16 | DLE | Data link escape | ctrl P | |
| 11 | 17 | DC1 | Device control 1 | ctrl Q | also XON |
| 12 | 18 | DC2 | Device control 2 | ctrl R | |
| 13 | 19 | DC3 | Device control 3 | ctrl S | also XOF |
| 14 | 20 | DC4 | Device control 4 | ctrl T | |
| 15 | 21 | NAK | Negative acknowledge | ctrl U | |
| 16 | 22 | SYN | Synchronous Idle | ctrl V | |
| 17 | 23 | ETB | End trans. block | ctrl W | |
| 18 | 24 | CAN | Cancel | ctrl X | |
| 19 | 25 | EM | End medium | ctrl Y | |
| 1A | 26 | SS | Special sequence | ctrl Z | spare |
| 1B | 27 | ESC | Escape | check manuals to transmit | |
| 1C | 28 | FS | File separator | | |
| 1D | 29 | GS | Group separator | | |
| 1E | 30 | RS | Record separator | | |
| 1F | 31 | US | Unit separator | | |
| 20 | 32 | SP | Space | | |
| 21 | 33 | ! | | | |
| 22 | 34 | " | | | |
| 23 | 35 | # | | £ | |
| 24 | 36 | $ | | | |
| 25 | 37 | % | | | |
| 26 | 38 | & | | | |
| 27 | 39 | ' | Apostrophe | | |
| 28 | 40 | ( | | | |
| 29 | 41 | ) | | | |
| 2A | 42 | * | | | |
| 2B | 43 | + | | | |
| 2C | 44 | , | Comma | | |
| 2D | 45 | - | | | |
| 2E | 46 | . | Period | | |
| 2F | 47 | / | Slash | | |
| 30 | 48 | 0 | | | |
| 31 | 49 | 1 | | | |
| 32 | 50 | 2 | | | |
| 33 | 51 | 3 | | | |
| 34 | 52 | 4 | | | |
| 35 | 53 | 5 | | | |
| 36 | 54 | 6 | | | |
| 37 | 55 | 7 | | | |

| HEX | DEC | ASCII | Name | Keyboard | Notes |
|-----|-----|-------|------|----------|-------|
| 38 | 56 | 8 | | | |
| 39 | 57 | 9 | | | |
| 3A | 58 | : | Colon | | |
| 3B | 59 | ; | Semi-colon | | |
| 3C | 60 | < | | | |
| 3D | 61 | = | | | |
| 3E | 62 | > | | | |
| 3F | 63 | ? | | | |
| 40 | 64 | @ | | | |
| 41 | 65 | A | | | |
| 42 | 66 | B | | | |
| 43 | 67 | C | | | |
| 44 | 68 | D | | | |
| 45 | 69 | E | | | |
| 46 | 70 | F | | | |
| 47 | 71 | G | | | |
| 48 | 72 | H | | | |
| 49 | 73 | I | | | |
| 4A | 74 | J | | | |
| 4B | 75 | K | | | |
| 4C | 76 | L | | | |
| 4D | 77 | M | | | |
| 4E | 78 | N | | | |
| 4F | 79 | O | | | |
| 50 | 80 | P | | | |
| 51 | 81 | Q | | | |
| 52 | 82 | R | | | |
| 53 | 83 | S | | | |
| 54 | 84 | T | | | |
| 55 | 85 | U | | | |
| 56 | 86 | V | | | |
| 57 | 87 | W | | | |
| 58 | 88 | X | | | |
| 59 | 89 | Y | | | |
| 5A | 90 | Z | | | |
| 5B | 91 | [ | | | |
| 5C | 92 | \ | Backslash | | |
| 5D | 93 | ] | | | |
| 5E | 94 | ^ | Circumflex | | |
| 5F | 95 | — | Underscore | | |
| 60 | 96 | | Grave accent | | |
| 61 | 97 | a | | | |
| 62 | 98 | b | | | |

| HEX | DEC | ASCII Name | Keyboard | Notes |
|-----|-----|------------|----------|-------|
| 63 | 99 | c | | |
| 64 | 100 | d | | |
| 65 | 101 | e | | |
| 66 | 102 | f | | |
| 67 | 103 | g | | |
| 68 | 104 | h | | |
| 69 | 105 | i | | |
| 6A | 106 | j | | |
| 6B | 107 | k | | |
| 6C | 108 | l | | |
| 6D | 109 | m | | |
| 6E | 110 | n | | |
| 6F | 111 | o | | |
| 70 | 112 | p | | |
| 71 | 113 | q | | |
| 72 | 114 | r | | |
| 73 | 115 | s | | |
| 74 | 116 | t | | |
| 75 | 117 | u | | |
| 76 | 118 | v | | |
| 77 | 119 | w | | |
| 78 | 120 | x | | |
| 79 | 121 | y | | |
| 7A | 122 | z | | |
| 7B | 123 | { | | |
| 7C | 124 | \| | | |
| 7D | 125 | } | | |
| 7E | 126 | ~   Tilde | | |
| 7F | 127 | DEL   Delete | | |

**Baudot**

This is the telex/telegraphy code known to the CCITT as International Alphabet No 2. It is essentially a 5-bit code, bracketed by a start bit (space) and a stop bit (mark). Idling is shown by 'mark'. The code only supports capital letters, figures and two 'supervisory' codes: 'Bell' to warn the operator at the far end and 'WRU' — 'Who are you?' to interrogate the far end. 'Figures' changes all characters received after to their alternates, and 'Letters' switches back. The letters/figures shift is used to give the entire character set.

Start – Stop Signal Code

| | | | |
|---|---|---|---|
| A | — | ○●●○○○● | |
| B | ? | ○●○○○●● | |
| C | : | ○○●●●○● | |
| D | Who Are You | ○●○○●○● | |
| E | 3 | ○●○○○○● | |
| F | % | ○●○○●●● | |
| G | @ | ○○●○●●● | |
| H | £ | ○○○●●○● | |
| I | 8 | ○○●●○○● | |
| J | Bell | ○○●○●○● | |
| K | ( | ○●●●●○● | |
| L | ) | ○○●○○●● | |
| M | . | ○○○●●●● | |
| N | , | ○○○●●○● | |
| O | 9 | ○○○○●●● | |

| | | | |
|---|---|---|---|
| P | 0 | ○○●●○●● | |
| Q | 1 | ○●●●●○● | |
| R | 4 | ○○●○●○● | |
| S | ' | ○●○●○○● | |
| T | 5 | ○○○○○●● | |
| U | 7 | ○●●●○○● | |
| V | = | ○○●●●●● | |
| W | 2 | ○●●●○○● | |
| X | / | ○●○●●●● | |
| Y | 6 | ○●○●○●● | |
| Z | + | ○●○○○●● | |
| Carriage Return | | ○○○○●○● | |
| Figures | | ○●●○●●● | |
| Letters | | ○●●●●●● | |
| Line Feed | | ○○●○○○● | |

Space   ○○○●○○●

Key :–  ● Marking Signal
        ○ Spacing Signal

## Viewdata

This is the character set used by the UK system, which is the most widely used, world-wide. The character-set has many features in common with ASCII but also departs from it in significant ways, notably to provide various forms of graphics, colour controls, screen-clear (ctrl L) etc. The set is shared with teletext which in itself requires further special codes, e.g. to enable sub-titling to broadcast television, newsflash etc.

If you are using proper viewdata software, then everything will display properly; if you are using a conventional terminal emulator then the result may look confusing.

Each character consists of 10 bits:

| | |
|---|---|
| Start | binary 0 |
| 7 bits of character code | |
| Parity bit | even |
| Stop | binary 1 |

ENQ (Ctrl E) is sent by the host on log-on to initiate the auto-log-on from the user's terminal. If no response is obtained, the user is requested to input the password manually. Each new page sequence opens with a clear screen instruction (Ctrl L, CHR$12) followed by a home (Ctrl M, CHR$14).

Some viewdata services are also available via standard asynchronous 300/300 ports (Prestel is, for example); in these cases, the graphics characters are stripped out and replaced by ****s; and the pages will scroll up the screen rather than present themselves in the frame-by-frame format.

# TABLE 2A PRESTEL TRANSMISSION CODES

| bits b7 b6 b5 → | 0 (000) | 1 (001) | 2 (010) | 3 (011) | 3b | 4 (100) | 4b | 5 (101) | 5b | 6 (110) | 7 (111) |
|---|---|---|---|---|---|---|---|---|---|---|---|
| **b4 b3 b2 b1 / ROW** | CO | | | | | | | | | | |
| 0000 — 0 | NUL | | SP | 0 | | @ | | P | | — | p |
| 0001 — 1 | | CURSOR ON | ! | 1 | SE VERIFY MODE (1) | A | ALPHANUMERIC RED | Q | MOSAIC RED | a | q |
| 0010 — 2 | | | " | 2 | SET VERIFY MODE (2) | B | ALPHANUMERIC GREEN | R | MOSAIC GREEN | b | r |
| 0011 — 3 | | CURSOR OFF | £ | 3 | SKIP BLOCK | C | ALPHANUMERIC BLUE | S | MOSAIC YELLOW | c | s |
| 0100 — 4 | | | $ | 4 | SET PROGRAMME MODE | D | ALPHANUMERIC YELLOW | T | MOSAIC BLUE | d | t |
| 0101 — 5 | ENQ | | % | 5 | | E | ALPHANUMERIC MAGENTA | U | MOSAIC MAGENTA | e | u |
| 0110 — 6 | | | & | 6 | | F | ALPHANUMERIC CYAN | V | MOSAIC CYAN | f | v |
| 0111 — 7 | | | ' | 7 | | G | ALPHANUMERIC WHITE | W | MOSAIC WHITE | g | w |
| 1000 — 8 | ACTIVE POSITION BACKWARD (APB) | | ( | 8 | | H | FLASH | X | CONCEAL DISPLAY | h | x |
| 1001 — 9 | ACTIVE POSITION FORWARD (APF) | | ) | 9 | | I | STEADY | Y | CONTIGUOUS MOSAICS | i | y |
| 1010 — 10 | ACTIVE POSITION DOWN (APD) | | * | : | | J | | Z | SEPARATED MOSAICS | j | z |
| 1011 — 11 | ACTIVE POSITION UP (APU) | ESC | + | ; | | K | | ← | | k | ¼ |
| 1100 — 12 | CLEAR SCREEN (CLS) | | , | < | | L | NORMAL HEIGHT | ½ | BLACK BACKGROUND | l | ‖ |
| 1101 — 13 | ACTIVE POSITION RETURN (APR) | | - | = | | M | DOUBLE HEIGHT | → | NEW BACKGROUND | m | ¾ |
| 1110 — 14 | ACTIVE POSITION HOME (APH) | | . | > | | N | | ↑ | HOLD MOSAICS | n | ÷ |
| 1111 — 15 | | | / | ? | | O | | # | RELEASE MOSAICS | o | █ |

NOTE:

COLUMNS 0 AND 1 FORM THE CO CONTROL CHARACTER SET

COLUMNS 4B AND 5B FORM THE C1 SET OF DISPLAY ATTRIBUTE CONTROL CODES

COLUMNS 2,3,4,5,6, AND 7 FORM THE GO CHARACTER SET

COLUMNS 2A, 3A, 4,5, 6A AND 7A FORM THE MOSAIC CHARACTER SET. THE SHADED AREA REPRESENTS FOREGROUND COLOUR.

If you wish to edit to a viewdata system using a normal keyboard, or view a viewdata stream as it comes from a host using 'control-show' facilities, the table below gives the usual equivalents. The normal default at the left-hand side of each line is alphanumerics white. Each subsequent 'attribute', ie if you wish to change to colour, or a variety of graphics, occupies a character space. Routing commands and signals to start and end edit depend on the software installed on the viewdata host computer: in Prestel compatible systems, the edit page is *910#, options must be entered in lower case letters and end edit is called by <esc>K.

| esc A | alpha red | esc Q | graphics red |
| esc B | alpha green | esc R | graphics green |
| esc C | alpha yellow | esc S | graphics yellow |
| esc D | alpha blue | esc T | graphics blue |
| esc E | alpha magenta | esc U | graphics magenta |
| esc F | alpha cyan | esc V | graphics cyan |
| esc G | alpha white | esc W | graphics white |
| esc H | flash | esc I | steady |
| esc L | normal height | esc M | double height |
| esc Y | contiguous graphics | esc Z | separated graphics |
| esc ctrl D | black background | esc-shift M | new background (varies) |
| esc J | start edit | esc K | end edit |

## EBCDIC

The Extended Binary Coded Decimal Interchange Code is a 256-state 8-bit extended binary coded digit code employed by IBM for internal purposes and is the only important exception to ASCII. Not all 256 codes are utilised, being reserved for future expansion, and a number are specially identified for application-specific purposes. In transmission, it is usual to add a further digit for parity checking. Normally the transmission mode is synchronous, so there are no 'start' and 'stop' bits.

The table shows how EBCDIC compares with ASCII of the same bit configuration.

## IBM control characters:

| EBCDIC | bits | Notes |
|---|---|---|
| NUL | 0000 0000 | Nul |
| SOH | 0000 0001 | Start of Heading |
| STX | 0000 0010 | Start of Text |
| ETX | 0000 0011 | End of Text |
| PF | 0000 0100 | Punch Off |
| HT | 0000 0101 | Horizontal Tab |
| LC | 0000 0110 | Lower Case |
| DEL | 0000 0111 | Delete |
|  | 0000 1000 |  |
| RLF | 0000 1001 | Reverse Line Feed |
| SMM | 0000 1010 | Start of Manual Message |
| VT | 0000 1011 | Vertical Tab |
| FF | 0000 1100 | Form Feed |
| CR | 0000 1101 | Carriage Return |
| SO | 0000 1110 | Shift Out |
| SI | 0000 1111 | Shift In |
| DLE | 0001 0000 | Data Link Exchange |
| DC1 | 0001 0001 | Device Control 1 |
| DC2 | 0001 0010 | Device Control 2 |
| TM | 0001 0011 | Tape Mark |
| RES | 0001 0100 | Restore |
| NL | 0001 0101 | New Line |
| BS | 0001 0110 | Back Space |
| IL | 0001 0111 | Idle |
| CAN | 0001 1000 | Cancel |
| EM | 0001 1001 | End of Medium |
| CC | 0001 1010 | Cursor Control |
| CU1 | 0001 1011 | Customer Use 1 |
| IFS | 0001 1100 | Interchange File Separator |
| IGS | 0001 1101 | Interchange Group Separator |
| IRS | 0001 1110 | Interchange Record Separator |
| IUS | 0001 1111 | Interchange Unit Separator |
| DS | 0010 0000 | Digit Select |
| SOS | 0010 0001 | Start of Significance |
| FS | 0010 0010 | Field Separator |
|  | 0010 0011 |  |
| BYP | 0010 0100 | Bypass |
| LF | 0010 0101 | Line Feed |
| ETB | 0010 0110 | End of Transmission Block |

| EBCDIC | bits | | Notes |
|---|---|---|---|
| ESC | 0010 | 0111 | Escape |
| | 0010 | 1000 | |
| | 0010 | 1001 | |
| SM | 0010 | 1010 | Set Mode |
| CU2 | 0010 | 1011 | Customer Use 1 |
| | 0010 | 1100 | |
| ENQ | 0010 | 1101 | Enquiry |
| ACK | 0010 | 1110 | Acknowledge |
| BEL | 0010 | 1111 | Bell |
| | 0011 | 0000 | |
| | 0011 | 0001 | |
| SYN | 0011 | 0010 | Synchronous Idle |
| | 0011 | 0011 | |
| PN | 0011 | 0100 | Punch On |
| RS | 0011 | 0101 | Reader Stop |
| UC | 0011 | 0110 | Upper Case |
| EOT | 0011 | 0111 | End of Transmission |
| | 0011 | 1000 | |
| | 0011 | 1001 | |
| | 0011 | 1010 | |
| CU3 | 0011 | 1011 | Customer Use 3 |
| DC4 | 0011 | 1100 | Device Control 4 |
| NAK | 0011 | 1101 | Negative Acknowledge |
| | 0011 | 1110 | |
| SUB | 0011 | 1111 | Substitute |
| SP | 0100 | 0000 | Space |

# Modems and Services

The table below shows all but two of the types of service you are likely to come across; V-designators are the world-wide 'official names given by the CCITT; Bell-designators are the US names:

| Service Designator | Speed | Duplex | Transmit 0 | Transmit 1 | Receive 0 | Receive 1 | Answer |
|---|---|---|---|---|---|---|---|
| V21 orig | 300* | full | 1180 | 980 | 1850 | 1650 | 8— |
| V21 ans | 300* | full | 1850 | 1650 | 1180 | 980 | 2100 |
| V23 (1) | 600 | half | 1700 | 1300 | 1700 | 1300 | 2100 |
| V23 (2) | 1200 | f/h† | 2100 | 1300 | 2100 | 1300 | 2100 |
| V23 back | 75 | f/h† | 450 | 390 | 450 | 390 | — |
| Bell 103 orig | 300* | full | 1070 | 1270 | 2025 | 2225 | — |
| Bell 103 ans | 300* | full | 2025 | 2225 | 1070 | 1270 | 2225 |
| Bell 202 | 1200 | half | 2200 | 1200 | 2200 | 1200 | 2025 |

* any speed up to 300 baud, can also include 75 and 110 baud services

† service can either be half-duplex at 1200 baud or asymmetrical full duplex, with 75 baud originate and 1200 baud receive (commonly used as viewdata user) or 1200 transmit and 75 receive (viewdata host)

The two exceptions are:
V22        1200 baud full duplex, two wire
Bell 212A   The US equivalent
Both these services operate by detecting phase as well as tone.

British Telecom markets the UK services under the name of Datel as follows — for simplicity The list covers only those services which use the PTSN or are otherwise easily accessible — 4-wire services, for example are excluded.

| Datel | Speed | Mode | Remarks |
|-------|-------|------|---------|
| 100(H) | 50 | async | Teleprinters, Baudot code |
| 100(J) | 75-110 | async | News services etc, Baudot code |
| | 50 | async | Telex service, Baudot code |
| 200 | 300 | async | full duplex, ASCII |
| 400 | 600 Hz | async | out-station to in-station only |
| 600 | 1200 | async | several versions exist — for 1200 half-duplex; 75/1200 for viewdata users; 1200/75 for viewdata hosts; and a rare 600 variant. The 75 speed is technically only for supervision but gives asymmetrical duplex |

BT has supplied the following modems for the various services — the older ones are now available on the 'second-user' market:

| Modem No | Remarks |
|----------|---------|
| 1 | 1200 half-duplex — massive |
| 2 | 300 full-duplex — massive |
| 11 | 4800 synchronous — older type |
| 12 | 2400/1200 synchronous |
| 13 | 300 full-duplex — plinth type |
| 20(1) | 1200 half-duplex — 'shoe-box' style |
| (2) | 1200/75 asymetrical duplex — 'shoe-box' style |
| (3) | 75/1200 asymetrical duplex — 'shoe-box' style |
| 21 | 300 full-duplex — modern type |
| 22 | 1200 half-duplex — modern type |
| 24 | 4800 synchronous — modern type (made by Racal) |
| 27A | 1200 full duplex, sync or async (US made & modified from Bell 212A to CCITT tones) |
| 27B | 1200 full duplex, sync or async (UK made) |

You should note that some commercial 1200/1200 full duplex modems also contain firmware providing ARQ error correction protocols; modems on both ends of the line must have the facilities, of course.

## BT Line Connectors

Modems can be connected directly to the BT network ('hard-wired') simply by identifying the pair that comes into the building. Normally the pair you want are the two outer wires in a standard 4 x 2 BT junction box. (The other wires are the 'return' or to support a 'ringing' circuit.)

A variety of plugs and sockets have been used by BT. Until recently, the standard connector for a modem was a 4-ring jack, type 505, to go into a socket 95A. Prestel equipment was terminated into a similar jack, this time with 5 rings, which went into a socket type 96A. However, now all phones, modems, viewdata sets etc, are terminated in the identical modular jack, type 600. The corresponding sockets need special tools to insert the line cable into the appropriate receptacles. Whatever other inter-connections you see behind a socket, the two wires of the twisted pair are the ones found in the centres of the two banks of receptacles.

North America also now uses a modular jack and socket system, but not one which is physically compatible with UK designs...did you expect otherwise?

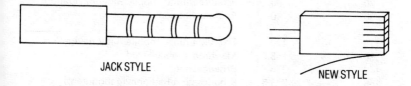

JACK STYLE

NEW STYLE

# The Radio Spectrum

The table gives the allocation of the radio frequency spectrum up to 30 MHz. The bands in which radio-teletype and radio-data traffic are most common are those allocated to 'fixed' services, but data traffic is also found in the amateur and maritime bands.

## VLF,MF,HF, RADIO FREQUENCY SPECTRUM TABLE

| | | | |
|---|---|---|---|
| 9 | — | 14 | Radionavigation |
| 14 | — | 19.95 | Fixed/Maritime mobile |
| 20 | | | Standard Frequency & Time |
| 20.05 | — | 70 | Fixed & Maritime mobile |
| 70 | — | 90 | Fixed/Maritime mobile/Radionavigation |
| 90 | — | 110 | Radionavigation |
| 110 | — | 130 | Fixed/Maritime mobile/Radionavigation |
| 130 | — | 148.5 | Maritime mobile/Fixed |
| 148.5 | — | 255 | Broadcasting |
| 255 | — | 283.5 | Broadcasting/Radionavigation(aero) |
| 283.5 | — | 315 | Maritime/Aeronautical navigation |
| 315 | — | 325 | Aeronautical radionavigation/Maritime radiobeacons |
| 325 | — | 405 | Aeronautical radionavigation |
| 405 | — | 415 | Radionavigation (410 = DF) |
| 415 | — | 495 | Aeronautical radionavigation/Maritime mobile |
| 495 | — | 505 | Mobile (distress & calling) > 500:cw&rtty |
| 505 | — | 526.5 | Maritime mobile/Aeronautical navigation |
| 526.5 | — | 1606.5 | Broadcasting |
| 1606.5 | — | 1625 | Maritime mobile/Fixed/Land mobile |
| 1625 | — | 1635 | Radiolocation |
| 1635 | — | 1800 | Maritime mobile/Fixed/Land mobile |
| 1800 | — | 1810 | Radiolocation |
| 1810 | — | 1850 | Amateur |
| 1850 | — | 2000 | Fixed/Mobile |

| | | | |
|---|---|---|---|
| 2000 | — | 2045 | Fixed/Mobile |
| 2045 | — | 2160 | Maritime mobile/Fixed/Land mobile |
| 2160 | — | 2170 | Radiolocation |
| 2170 | — | 2173.5 | Maritime mobile |
| 2173.5 | — | 2190.5 | Mobile (distress & calling) >2182 — voice |
| 2190.5 | — | 2194 | Maritime & Mobile |
| 2194 | — | 2300 | Fixed & Mobile |
| 2300 | — | 2498 | Fixed/Mobile/Broadcasting |
| 2498 | — | 2502 | Standard Frequency & Time |
| 2502 | — | 2650 | Maritime mobile/Maritime radionavigation |
| 2650 | — | 2850 | Fixed/Mobile |
| 2850 | — | 3025 | Aeronautical mobile (R) |
| 3025 | — | 3155 | Aeronautical mobile (OR) |
| 3155 | — | 3200 | Fixed/Mobile/Low power hearing aids |
| 3200 | — | 3230 | Fixed/Mobile/Broadcasting |
| 3230 | — | 3400 | Fixed/Mobile/Broadcasting |
| 3400 | — | 3500 | Aeronautical mobile (R) |
| 3500 | — | 3800 | Amateur/Fixed/Mobile |
| 3800 | — | 3900 | Fixed/Aeronautical mobile (OR) |
| 3900 | — | 3930 | Aeronautical mobile (OR) |
| 3930 | — | 4000 | Fixed/Broadcasting |
| 4000 | — | 4063 | Fixed/Maritime mobile |
| 4063 | — | 4438 | Maritime mobile |
| 4438 | — | 4650 | Fixed/Mobile |
| 4650 | — | 4700 | Aeronautical mobile (R) |
| 4700 | — | 4750 | Aeronautical mobile (OR) |
| 4750 | — | 4850 | Fixed/Aeronautical mobile (OR)/ Land mobile/Broadcasting |
| 4850 | — | 4995 | Fixed/Land mobile/Broadcasting |
| 4995 | — | 5005 | Standard Frequency & Time |
| 5005 | — | 5060 | Fixed/Broadcasting |
| 5060 | — | 5450 | Fixed/Mobile |
| 5450 | — | 5480 | Fixed/Aeronautical mobile (OR)/Land mobile |
| 5480 | — | 5680 | Aeronautical mobile (R) |
| 5680 | — | 5730 | Aeronautical mobile (OR) |
| 5730 | — | 5950 | Fixed/Land mobile |
| 5950 | — | 6200 | Broadcasting |
| 6200 | — | 6525 | Maritime mobile |
| 6525 | — | 6685 | Aeronautical mobile (R) |
| 6685 | — | 6765 | Aeronautical mobile (OR) |
| 6765 | — | 6795 | Fixed/ISM |
| 7000 | — | 7100 | Amateur |
| 7100 | — | 7300 | Broadcasting |
| 7300 | — | 8100 | Maritime mobile |

| | | | |
|---|---|---|---|
| 8100 | — | 8195 | Fixed/Maritime mobile |
| 8195 | — | 8815 | Maritime mobile |
| | | | |
| 8815 | — | 8965 | Aeronautical mobile (R) |
| 8965 | — | 9040 | Aeronautical mobile (OR) |
| 9040 | — | 9500 | Fixed |
| 9500 | — | 9900 | Broadcasting |
| 9900 | — | 9995 | Fixed |
| | | | |
| 9995 | — | 10005 | Standard Frequency & Time |
| 10005 | — | 10100 | Aeronautical mobile (R) |
| 10100 | — | 10150 | Fixed/Amateur(sec) |
| 10150 | — | 11175 | Fixed |
| 11175 | — | 11275 | Aeronautical mobile (OR) |
| 11275 | — | 11400 | Aeronautical mobile (R) |
| 11400 | — | 11650 | Fixed |
| | | | |
| 11650 | — | 12050 | Broadcasting |
| 12050 | — | 12230 | Fixed |
| 12230 | — | 13200 | Maritime mobile |
| | | | |
| 13200 | — | 13260 | Aeronautical mobile (OR) |
| 13260 | — | 13360 | Aeronautical mobile (R) |
| 13360 | — | 13410 | Fixed/Radio Astronomy |
| 13410 | — | 13600 | Fixed |
| 13600 | — | 13800 | Broadcasting |
| 13800 | — | 14000 | Fixed |
| | | | |
| 14000 | — | 14350 | Amateur |
| 14350 | — | 14990 | Fixed |
| | | | |
| 14990 | — | 15010 | Standard Frequency & Time |
| 15010 | — | 15100 | Aeronautical mobile (OR) |
| 15100 | — | 15600 | Broadcasting |
| 15600 | — | 16360 | Fixed |
| | | | |
| 16360 | — | 17410 | Maritime mobile |
| 17410 | — | 17550 | Fixed |
| 17550 | — | 17900 | Broadcasting |
| 17900 | — | 17970 | Aeronautical mobile (R) |
| 17970 | — | 18030 | Aeronautical mobile (OR) |
| | | | |
| 18030 | — | 18052 | Fixed |
| 18052 | — | 18068 | Fixed/Space Research |
| 18068 | — | 18168 | Amateur |
| 18168 | — | 18780 | Fixed |
| 18780 | — | 18900 | Maritime mobile |
| 18900 | — | 19680 | Fixed |

| | | | |
|---|---|---|---|
| 19680 | — | 19800 | Maritime mobile |
| 19800 | — | 19990 | Fixed |
| | | | |
| 19990 | — | 20010 | Standard Frequency & Time |
| 20010 | — | 21000 | Fixed |
| 21000 | — | 21450 | Amateur |
| 21450 | — | 21850 | Broadcasting |
| 21850 | — | 21870 | Fixed |
| 21870 | — | 21924 | Aeronautical fixed |
| 21924 | — | 22000 | Aeronautical (R) |
| | | | |
| 22000 | — | 22855 | Maritime mobile |
| 22855 | — | 23200 | Fixed |
| 23200 | — | 23350 | Aeronautical fixed & mobile (R) |
| 23350 | — | 24000 | Fixed/Mobile |
| 24000 | — | 24890 | Fixed/Land mobile |
| | | | |
| 24890 | — | 24990 | Amateur |
| 24990 | — | 25010 | Standard Frequency & Time |
| 25010 | — | 25070 | Fixed/Mobile |
| 25070 | — | 25210 | Maritime mobile |
| 25210 | — | 25550 | Fixed/Mobile |
| 25550 | — | 25670 | Radio Astronomy |
| | | | |
| 25670 | — | 26100 | Broadcasting |
| 26100 | — | 26175 | Maritime mobile |
| 26175 | — | 27500 | Fixed/Mobile (CB) (26.975-27.2835 ISM) |
| 27500 | — | 28000 | Meteorological aids/Fixed/Mobile (CB) |
| 28000 | — | 29700 | Amateur |
| 29700 | — | 30005 | Fixed/Mobile |

**Note:** These allocations are as they apply in Europe, slight variations occur in other regions of the globe.

# Port-finder Flowchart

This flow-chart will enable owners of auto-diallers to carry out an automatic search of a range of telephone numbers to determine which of them have modems hanging off the back.

It's a flow-chart and not a program listing, because the whole exercise is very hardware dependent: you will have to determine what sort of instructions your auto-modem will accept, and in what form; you must also see what sort of signals it can send back to your computer so that your program can 'read' them.

You will also need to devise some ways of sensing the phone line, whether it has been seized, whether you are getting 'ringing', if there is an engaged tone, a voice, a number obtainable tone, or a modem whistle. Line seizure detect, if not already available on your modem, is simply a question of reading the phone line voltage; the other conditions can be detected with simple tone decoder modules based on the 567 chip.

The lines from these detectors should then be brought to a A/D board which your computer software can scan and read.

# PORT FINDER FLOW CHART

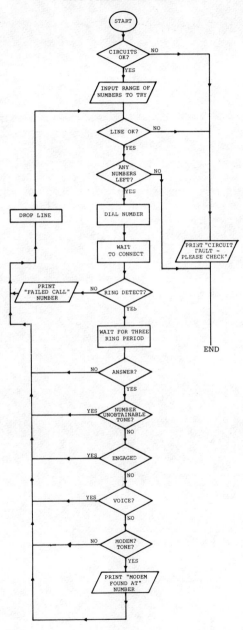

START

CIRCUITS OK? — NO

YES

INPUT RANGE OF NUMBERS TO TRY

LINE OK? — NO

YES

ANY NUMBERS LEFT? — NO

YES

DIAL NUMBER

WAIT TO CONNECT

RING DETECT? — NO → PRINT "FAILED CALL" NUMBER

YES

WAIT FOR THREE RING PERIOD

ANSWER? — NO

YES

NUMBER UNOBTAINABLE TONE? — YES

NO

ENGAGED? — YES

NO

VOICE? — YES

NO

MODEM? TONE? — NO

YES

PRINT "MODEM FOUND AT" NUMBER

DROP LINE

PRINT "CIRCUIT FAULT – PLEASE CHECK"

END